What Leaders are Saying

"The most profound shifts in marketing start with a profound shift in buying. We are in an important phase of that shift, where general practitioners accept the extreme empowerment granted to buyers. Yet, they struggle to adapt quickly. Dave Sutton's *Marketing, Interrupted* is the new book for our age. Anyone in an executive leadership role will take home insights to help them accelerate their transformation and improve the advocacy of their brand."

—Mark Roberge,
Senior Lecturer at Harvard Business School, Former CRO at HubSpot

"Dave provides a brilliant blueprint for connecting the dots in our collective journey to making brands positive solutions in people's lives. In a consumer-first world, he simplifies the transformational power of business to engage in authentic relationships with people."

—Ed Farley,
former CMO United Way

"When asked to review this new marketing book, I hesitated. Will it have a new message for marketers? Will it be well-written? Will it contain fresh marketing stories? Will it cover all the new developments in marketing? My answer is Yes! Read Dave Sutton's *Marketing, Interrupted*!"

—Phil Kotler, S.C.Johnson ,
Distinguished Professor of International Marketing
at Northwestern University

"Dave Sutton possesses a brilliant, innovative mind and is at the forefront of anticipating global marketing trends with remarkable precision and this book will prove him right once again."

—Lidia Frayne,
Chief of Staff, Digital Marketing, Dell

"*Marketing, Interrupted* is a must-read for any business leader who is under pressure to get results from their company's marketing efforts. Dave Sutton had me glued from the beginning because he shows how Transformational Marketing is built on a foundation of intimate knowledge of the customer, which is the basis of everything I've ever done as a marketing leader, industry analyst, and entrepreneur. Only then can you stand out, yet so many companies are shooting in the dark. If you're ready to have your current thinking about marketing interrupted, read this book."

—Jeff Ernst,

CEO SlapFive; ex-CMO Forrester Research

"*Marketing, Interrupted* touches on one of the most crucial issues facing marketers today. You have to stay relevant to your customers and meet them where they are. Dave's book crystalizes how today's marketers must evolve to do just that."

—Steve Lucas,

CEO, Marketo

"Love this book. It enters my list of "go-to" thought leadership in marketing. We are enjoying a time when marketers cannot plug'n play anymore. To be successful, the CMO must be ready to call the audible at the line of scrimmage. That means building a team that can process meaning on the fly, not just formulas for message, reach and frequency!"

—Tim McMahon,

Culture, Leadership & Learning Officer, JetLinx Aviation

"One Voice. One Look. One Story – *Marketing, Interrupted* is beautifully explained through interesting story telling. A book hard to put down as each story teaches a lesson in marketing yet simply told with facts."

—Umaesh Khaitan,

CEO Door Kraft Products

"*Marketing, Interrupted* is a much needed treatise on how to transform marketing from being mechanically business-focused to being truly customer-focused. Dave Sutton reminds us that our brand, our products, and our services are not really the hero. Our customers are. In this new media age, in which marketers just try to shout above everyone else, Dave interrupts the noise to get back to the basics of building meaning and trust through delivering on our brand promise. As both a for-profit and non-profit entrepreneur, this exciting new book is just what I needed right now."

—Chad Thevenot,
Executive Director IHS

"Global business is going through enormous transformation fueled by digital technologies. *Marketing, Interrupted* teaches you how to transform marketing and build brand power by applying a lens of simplicity, clarity and alignment"

—Fredrik Angelo Lindqvist,
CEO, Flowfactory

"If you need creativity in your company's kitchen, you can't get upset about burnt pancakes. *Marketing, Interrupted* highlights how storytelling can give more meaning to all of your employees and ultimately win over new talent. Bon appetit."

—Tom Klein,
CMO, Mailchimp

"Dave is the first marketing guru who had the guts to challenge us to prune some things rather than continuing to expand marketing activities and spend... brilliant and thanks!"

—Jim Brady,
President and CEO, Brady Services

"An insightful and scholarly book that will serve as a reminder to the marketing community that real Transformation is first and foremost about the People, the other P's come later. I've always known Dave as an "interrupter" who blends analytical reasoning and emotional cognitions to the delight of his audience."

—Harmandeep Singh,
Chief Strategy Officer, Building Clarity

"Love, love, love this book! It simplifies and provides evidence-based use cases for what marketers must do to successfully acquire new customers. Readers may comb through the book to find the right case study to create long-lasting relationships with customers. It is a must read for any marketer trying to build the brand story and create strategies to elevate an organization's marketing and branding efforts."

—Scott Klinger,
VP Marketing and eCommerce,
First Data Corporation

"This book is a compelling and entertaining guide to telling a brand's story in the 21st century, and what that means for strategy and systems, not just in the developed world but in emerging markets as well. 'Make the customer the hero' is one of the key ideas in this book, but it is perhaps the hardest thing for marketers to do. With the case studies and step-by-step advice in this book, marketers can deliver the kind of customer-centricity that will move them 'TopRight.' I highly recommend this book for business strategists ready to commit the time and money it takes nowadays to create enduring competitive advantage for their brands."

—J Walker Smith,
Chief Knowledge Officer, Brand and Marketing,
Kantar Consulting

"In this age of Digital Transformation, the role of marketing and the CMO continues to evolve. While tactics such as the digitization of the customer experience, the dematerialization of products into services and the advent of the platform economy, have altered corporate interactions, the basic tenets of marketing have not changed: driving innovation and growth by understanding and meeting the needs of the customer. Dave has masterfully captured and balanced the right tone between the strategy and tactics."

—Bill Hurley,
CMO, CenturyLink

"In *Marketing, Interrupted*, Dave Sutton has perfectly captured the nuance that goes into laying the necessary groundwork to successfully conveying a brand story in a way that consumers will care. This book does a tremendous job of helping marketers initiate meaningful conversations with customers that have longevity."

—Joe Koufman,
CEO and Founder, Agency Sparks

"Global business is going through enormous transformation fueled by digital technologies. *Marketing, Interrupted* teaches you how to transform marketing and build brand power by applying a lens of simplicity, clarity and alignment"

—Fredrik Angelo Lindqvist,
CEO, Flowfactory

"*Marketing, Interrupted* is a must-read for CEOs and marketers. It provides a roadmap for authentic conversations with customers that will lead to real 'Top-right' success."

—Slade Kobran,
CMO, Chief Outsiders

Marketing, Interrupted

**Sometimes the only way to succeed
is to go a little crazy**

Dave Sutton

Dav Sutto 5/2018

Top Right™

Portions of this manuscript have been previously published at Inc.com, TopRightPartners.com, and Entrepreneur.com

This is a publication of TopRight, LLC.

Publication services provided by Cause Communications, LLC. admin@causeco.co

To purchase this product in bulk for organizational purposes, contact TopRight, LLC at
678-384-6700.

ISBN: 978-1-945537-08-0 Hardcover
ISBN: 978-1-945537-09-7 Ebook

Printed in the United States of America

You know how it goes. You pick up a book, flip to the dedication, and find that, once again, the author has dedicated a book to someone else and not to you.

Not this time.

Because this book is for the passionate storytellers, the intellectually curious strategists, the modest marketing technologists… the unsung heroes, generating outsized returns for their companies every day.

This one's for you.

Contents

Part Three: Systems

Foreword

Jo Ann Herold

CMO of Honey Baked Ham

E very one of us has a great capacity for brilliance. That's my humble observa-tion from over 25 years working in marketing. Our brilliance translates to the products and services we sell, the people we serve, the stories we tell, and the experiences we create for our customers. It is true in any industry—transporta-tion, consumer goods, services or non-profit. It is also true for different divi-sions in business—sales, marketing, human resources, legal, finance, front-line or freelance.

But that brilliance is a moving target. Consumer demands change. Innovation, globalization, consolidation, increased transparency into our work and a never-ending need for ingenuity is the reality. Market shifts and disruptions are all over the world:

- Airbnb has become the largest hotel chain—without a single real-estate investment.

- Interface shrunk its carbon footprint and introduced green sustainabil-ity to the world.

- Netflix and other streaming services have reconfigured the entertain-ment industry.

- Uber has become the largest transportation company—without owning any vehicles.

- Amazon is shaking up the delivery space, redefining convenience and modernizing grocery shopping.

Transformation is all around us. There has never been a more exciting time to be in business, but the rulebooks of the yesteryear are no longer relevant.

All of this brings me to Dave Sutton's breakthrough book: *Marketing, Interrupted*. Dave is a great observer and synthesizer of trends and ideas, always on the cutting edge of the transformative and shifting business landscape. When we worked together at TopRight, I watched Dave help companies navigate the shifting sands of marketing, activating with our clients to give their customers a reason to buy, advocate and stay.

Dave has his finger on the pulse of disruptive strategies and ideas that are driving growth and change for the future. And he's a great storyteller. What I love about *Marketing, Interrupted* is how Dave shares real life examples of inspired business leaders and industries that are changing and growing. This book is inspiring, hopeful and optimistic, and reminds me of how much power we all have to change the world for the good. Don't we all want to be brave, stand out from the crowd and do something epic? Don't we all want to increase our capacity for brilliance?

This book is a roadmap for anyone who is trying to grow. These real-life stories and case studies provide optimism and hope for me in my field, but also for anyone who is trying to grow in the market place.

Marketing, Interrupted reminds us all how important our own ingenuity is. Dave teaches us how to tap into our ability to be the ultimate problem solver, be differentiated, tell great stories and create new experiences to engage in the marketplace and create a remarkable future.

Great marketers need one another. We need people who inspire us to lead, innovate and love our profession. Thank you, Dave, for inspiring me and the next generation based on purpose, values and love for marketing.

Introduction

Taylor Swift and Kanye West at the 2009
MTV Video Music Awards

Do you remember that famous (or infamous) moment at the 2009 MTV Video Music Awards?

Taylor Swift barely had accepted her award for Best Female Video when Kanye West rushed the stage, grabbed the microphone out of the startled teen's hands and launched into a crazy rant: "Yo, Taylor, I'm really happy for you and I'mma let you finish but Beyoncé had one of the best videos of all time. One of the best videos of all time!," the rapper said, referring to the undeniably danceable "Single Ladies."

Swift, who had won the award for her high school love song *You Belong With Me*, was, understandably, hurt.

"I was standing onstage, and I was really excited because I'd just won the award, and then I was really excited because Kanye West was onstage," she told *People* magazine. "And then I wasn't excited anymore after that."

This crazy interruption completely ruined the moment for Swift and stunned the audience. Nonetheless, songs from Taylor, Kanye and Beyoncé dominated the charts for weeks after the event and the sales for all three artists involved in this incident skyrocketed in the months that followed.

Seth Godin is famous for saying, "Finding new ways, more clever ways to interrupt people doesn't work." Is this a case where "interruptive" marketing pays off? Could Godin be wrong? If you continuously find new ways to shock and awe the audience, will it always pay off? Well, maybe in the entertainment industry or in politics (if your name is Donald Trump), but what about for the rest of us?

In the business world today, interruptive marketing may still work sometimes. However, in the long run, the odds are in favor of you losing your market when you trick or trap your audience as opposed to engaging them authentically. It just makes good business sense to market the way your customers want to be marketed to. Marketers must strive to work with their market, not against them.

The fact is that interruptive marketing—the continual pushing of brand messaging through traditional marketing methods, such as broadcast advertising, direct mail, display advertising, flashy booths at trade shows, and even sales people at times—is often just noise and nuisance. Your audience will go out of their way to avoid you.

Hugh MacLeod, the cartoonist who makes his living drawing "cube grenades" for his clients turns it up a notch by asserting, "If you talked to people the way advertising talked to people, they'd punch you in the face."

These conventional marketing methods have come under increased scrutiny and pressure to generate more consistent returns. Yet, the new reality is that marketing should speak *to* us, not *at* us. To achieve this requires an intimate knowledge of the customer. Only then can a brand stand out from the crowd and give customers a reason to listen, a reason to care and, most importantly, a reason to buy.

Sounds easy enough, doesn't it? Yet marketers are held to far higher standards today than they were just a few years ago. Every dollar spent on marketing is now being judged in terms of return on investment (ROI). Corporate executives, investors, shareholders and donors are evaluating marketing investment plans and portfolios in much the same way that other capital investments are made by the firm—demanding that marketing returns exceed the corporate "hurdle rate" for ROI.

This new era of marketing accountability calls for all marketers to design measurable go-to-market processes, actively monitor the performance of their marketing investments, and aggressively optimize marketing investment portfolios for true value creation, as seen through the eyes and responses of their customers. And in so doing, capture the "top right" position in their industry.

So, what exactly does it mean to be top right?

When industry analysts and strategic consultants model company performance within an industry, there is invariably a two-by-two matrix that is used to portray where each competitor stacks up in terms of performance. Whether the axes are revenue versus profitability or growth versus market share, it always seems to turn out that the place to be is in the top right corner of that two-by-two matrix.

The next question is how do you get there; how do you make that move to the top right corner of your industry or sector?

The answer: you have to transform the way you think about and execute your marketing.

Traditional marketers and advertisers continually try new and different ways to *interrupt us* as customers! And that's just not working anymore. It's inauthentic, ineffective, annoying and a waste of money. So, we're turning it around and using this book to *interrupt marketers* and challenge them to change their ways...

to transform marketing and give customers a reason to care, a reason to listen, a reason to engage, a reason to buy, and most importantly, a reason to stay.

Transformational Marketing literally transforms how your customer experiences you, understands you, and interacts with you. It is a change in mindset as well as methodology. No longer is the story simply about you and what you offer. Your brand, your products, your services are not really the hero.

The power and impact of your brand, your product, your services and your story comes from making the customer the hero, and you, the marketer, serving as the guide on their buying journey. Throughout the entire customer lifecycle, the intention—actually the requirement is to deliver on the brand promise. Only then will prospects become customers, and customers become brand advocates.

Why? Because Transformational Marketing is not simply about what you do. It is:

- Why you do what you do?

- What it is you do, based on that why?

- How you deliver it to your customers?

- What the impact is on their lives?

It is this impact that gives them a reason to care, a reason to buy, a reason to engage, a reason to stay. Top right companies routinely beat their competition and can even change the rules of the game as they become category leaders and category definers.

Transformational Marketing is how you move top right:

- Top right of your industry in terms of your financial performance

- Top right of setting the benchmark to which others aspire

- Top right of mind share and advocacy, where your customers don't just buy your products and services, they tell your story for you because your story matters to them

If you have the desire to win in the market, the patience to tolerate a little crazy, the endurance to drive to the top and the tenacity to stay there, then read on—this book is for you!

Congratulations! You're an ambitious marketer with a brand to build, leads to generate, revenue goals to hit and the ambition to be top right in your industry.

You've got a tremendous opportunity ahead of you to transform marketing and win in the markets where you compete, but a few obstacles may crop up along the way. This book is organized into three parts (the 3 S's) to help you identify, overcome and mitigate the associated risks of Transformational Marketing:

- **Part 1: Story:** A lack of timely, relevant customer insights to define a truly compelling yet simple story that connects with and engages your target audience

- **Part 2: Strategy:** An inability to clearly connect that story to your customers through formats that they consume, in channels that they use, across every touch point and at the right stage in their buying journey

- **Part 3: Systems:** Inability to align the necessary systems to flawlessly execute the strategy - with the supporting organization, culture, performance measures, data and technology

Avoiding or overcoming these obstacles is incredibly important. Why? Because they represent conditions for success—where you deliver on your promise and customers deliver on theirs in terms of paying for your product or service.

We have learned from experience that success among top right companies occurs when they excel in overcoming the three risks by telling a simple Story, creating a clear Strategy and aligning their Systems to execute with ruthless consistency.

The lens through which to evaluate marketing excellence is: Simplicity, Clarity, and Alignment. Any great brand that you can think of—from Apple to Zappos— has been built on the guiding principles of Simplicity, Clarity and Alignment: One Voice. One Look. One Story.

Simplicity in Story: The heart of Transformational Marketing is the story—a distillation of who you really are, a peeling back of the layers to discover "why" you do what you do and most importantly why that matters to your customer and how you deliver that value to them. This is the key to simplicity in your story.

Clarity in Strategy: One would think that having gone through the process of simplifying the complexities of your story, clarity automatically follows. But no, at least not without intentional and deliberate effort and process. Clarity speaks to the "what" of your story. What is it that you are actually doing, what is the value of your products and services and what impact will you achieve for your customers? You must be clear.

Simplicity and Clarity get you part of the way there, but as most marketers know, everything is a communications vehicle – inside and out. More often than not, if you stopped reading this right now and asked 10 co-workers to tell you the company story, you would get 10 different answers.

Alignment in Systems: Why? All of your marketing, all employee communications, all sales collateral, all enabling technologies, all of your people at every customer touchpoint must be fully aligned to bring your brand to life. As David Packard once said: "Marketing is too important to be left just to the marketing department." Alignment equates to the "how." How do your people communicate your story, how do you want your customers to experience your brand and how do you specifically deliver value? This is often where companies and organizations struggle the most.

Alignment sounds easy but is actually quite difficult to achieve, and even more difficult to sustain. It requires ruthless focus and consistency throughout your entire organization, both internally and then externally. Great brands only move to the top right if they are first understood, launched, and lived "inside-out."

Simply put: you can't have more than one Story; you can't have more than one Strategy to deliver that Story; and you need complete and total alignment of your organizational Systems to execute the Strategy. You must be fully aligned.

This is Transformational Marketing, this is how you move to the top right– the right Story, the right Strategy, the right Systems—all measured by looking through the lens of Simplicity, Clarity, and Alignment.

Chapter 1

Why Marketing Must Change

media.netflix.com

Hen Reed Hastings launched Netflix in August 1997, he was quoted as saying at the time that his goal for the business was, "not to provide DVD rentals through the Internet, but rather to allow for the best home video viewing for its customers." What an amazingly prescient statement from the founder of what is today the world's 10th-largest revenue-producing Internet company. Most people think of Netflix as an industry disrupter—the brand that would ultimately drive Blockbuster and many other retail video rental players out of business.

The Netflix brand story was simple and clear: greater video selection, more convenience than traveling to a video rental outlet and no late fees. Hastings was one of the first to see that the ability to personalize the shopper experience was a unique characteristic of the Internet. Hastings proclaimed that "if you can otherwise do it offline, people won't pay for it online. If our internet offering was going to be better than retail stores, we had to find something stores couldn't do well."

So, Netflix developed a recommendation algorithm driven by customer surveys and ratings, enabling them to offer the shopper recommendations for videos they might like based on what they had previously rented and enjoyed. This was a benefit that retail competitors like Blockbuster struggled to deliver. In contrast to Netflix, they had fragmented store systems and a general lack of insight into customer preferences, behaviors and commonalities across segments of the market.

Netflix software "learns" more about customers with every transaction and continuously makes relevant offers and refines recommendations based on deeper customer understanding. By transforming video rentals from a bricks and mortar retail experience to an online, personalized home delivery experience, Netflix gave its customers a compelling reason to listen, engage, buy and stay. Literally, Reed Hastings and his marketing team set the bar for a remarkable customer experience in the home entertainment industry.

However, the story doesn't stop there. Fast forward to 2007 and a company named Move Networks introduced a technology and service that once again would shake up the home entertainment industry: HTTP-based adaptive streaming. Why would you need to have a DVD delivered to your home overnight when you could have that same movie streamed instantly to your home through you set top cable box? The tables had turned! Now Netflix faced extinction as cable operators like Comcast and Cox Communications were reshaping the home entertainment experience and shifting customer expectations.

By all accounts, Netflix should have gone out of business at this time. How could they possibly compete? The Netflix brand story had been upstaged by a better story of selection, convenience and overall value. And if the company didn't change, it would cease to exist.

Fortunately for the company, Reed Hastings is a transformative leader, and as such, he always keeps his eye on the future. Introducing video on demand or streaming services for Netflix was not a question of "if" but "when." So, rather than roll over and file for bankruptcy, Hastings set out to mobilize his team to transform the business, formulate a new marketing strategy and develop the corresponding systems to compete, scale and win.

After all, the Netflix brand story had never been about *delivery of DVDs* to homes. It was about allowing for the ***best home video viewing*** for its customers. Over the next 12 months, the marketing team repositioned the brand from "overnight DVD delivery" to "instantaneous streaming video platform." Hastings and his team responded with an aggressive strategy to beat the cable players at their own game and make Netflix the world leader in streaming entertainment. Meanwhile, the Netflix technology team made sure that the systems were in place to execute the strategy and remain fully aligned on delivering the promise of the brand story. Today, Netflix boasts over 100 million monthly subscribers to their streaming service and they can instantaneously distribute content to any device, anywhere, anytime.

> *"I take pride in making as few decisions as possible. When you get to real scale, most of my job is just vision."*
> —Reed Hastings, Netflix founder and CEO

Thanks to the digital nature of streaming services, Netflix marketers were able to closely monitor viewer behaviors in search of insights. Early on, they noticed that subscribers were routinely binge-watching serial dramas –often consuming eight, ten, even twelve hours of episodes back-to-back. The most popular shows like HBO's "The Sopranos" were not only winning awards, they were winning the hearts and minds of the Netflix customer. Netflix perceived the content producers as both a threat and an opportunity. If a licensing deal fell apart with a large content producer like Disney, they might lose a chunk of their subscriber base. Given these circumstances, Reed Hastings determined that the best defense would be to go on the offense. By creating their own content, they could connect in a more relevant and sustained way with the subscriber.

As Netflix embarked on transforming itself into a content producer, they tapped into subscriber insights and focused on producing well-written, high-production value serial dramas like "House of Cards", "Stranger Things" and "Orange Is the New Black"—binge-worthy programming that would lock their subscribers in to the platform. These tremendously popular original productions are not only winning awards, they have accelerated the transformation of Netflix once again into a powerful, independent media company.

The series of successful transformations at Netflix is largely due to the leadership of Reed Hastings and the power of their simple, clear and fully aligned brand story. In addition, Netflix built a team of talented people, adept at reformulating strategies and quickly realigning systems to execute with ruthless consistency. For many brands today, the biggest barrier to success is their capacity to manage change and proactively transform their business—sometimes at the expense of disrupting what is currently a successful business model. Let's face it: the status quo is more comfortable. You can slip into cozy complacency and invest in a series of safe marketing initiatives that deliver "better sameness".

Consider the perspective of John Antioco, the former CEO at Blockbuster. He probably didn't think of Netflix as much of a threat when they first launched their DVD home delivery services. In 2004, Antioco oversaw an infrastructure that included over 9,000 store locations. Blockbuster was the "800-lb gorilla"- the category killer. Antioco probably thought that online video rentals represented a tiny, niche market—just focused on those "early adopters" of the Internet.

Transformational leaders like Reed Hastings have a general *discomfort with the status quo*. They continually challenge their people to "create the company that will put us out of business"—rather than waiting for some competitor to do it for them. They identify opportunities to transform how the customer experiences their brand story... more efficiently, conveniently, personalized, and that is exactly how companies like Netflix disrupt industry structures and avoid being disrupted by other new entrants.

What are the trends that drive brands like NetFlix to change?

The Netflix story is a perfect example of why marketing (and marketers) must change. We live and compete in a hyper competitive marketplace driven by an increasingly connected global economy and shaped by super savvy shoppers. These and other mega trends create the need for change in how marketers position their products and services in a diverse and dynamic marketplace. The big question is: How can businesses leverage these important trends as an opportunity to grow, to move to the TopRight quadrant in their competitive frame, and most importantly, to stay there?

There are so many trends and sub trends that may impact various industries that we could not possibly cover them all here. However, there are a few important trends that we believe will have an outsized effect on marketers in the next decade—driving innovation and transforming marketing to give customers a reason to care, a reason to listen, a reason to engage, a reason to buy and most importantly, a reason to stay.

The Emerging Middle Class: Welcome to the "next billions" market. According to estimate from the World Bank, the global middle class has grown from under two billion consumers in 2011 to nearly five billion within two decades, thanks to the economic growth in emerging markets. This tremendous new market is a key driver of growth and seeks for innovative products that may increase their quality of life. This consumer demographic trend is not only evident in emerging countries, but also in more developed countries. In US, for example, the increasing purchasing power of Hispanics, now eclipsing $1.2 trillion annually, directs marketer focus on attracting and engaging this lucrative segment with their brands. A share of wallet study from Nielsen shows that Hispanics spend at least $10 more per visit in consumer packaged goods than the total market.

> *"We are reaching a tipping point, where over the next several years the global middle class will expand dramatically."*
> —Hori Kharas, Brookings Institution

Regardless of the industry or category where you compete, transformative marketers must understand this emerging middle class, their wants and needs, their personalities and the distinctions in the ways they buy and consumer goods and services.

A New Form of Capitalism: Creating shared value is a new form of capitalism that works to generate positive results not only for the business, but also for the society. Shared value is not just about social responsibility, philanthropy, or even sustainability. It is a new way to achieve economic success by "reconceiving" products and markets in line with the society's needs such as health, better housing, improved nutrition, help for the aging, better use of scarce resources and less environmental damage. Literally overnight, brands are born and value is released from the marriage of scarce resource to a specific consumer need. Consider the simple and clear brand story of the mobile app JustPark: "Find parking in seconds." Users rent out their private parking spots to drivers in the local area who are looking to avoid exorbitant parking fees.

"We used to live in a world where there are people and a world where there are businesses, and now we're living in a world where people can become businesses in 60 seconds,"
—Brian Chesky, Co-founder of Airbnb

The sharing economy, led in large part by the Millennial generation, is now poised to disrupt traditional industry structures around the world. Consider how Uber, Airbnb and ZipCar have completely transformed the hospitality industry— these brands didn't even exist a decade ago. They've challenged big brand marketers at companies like Carey Limo, Hyatt and Avis to retrench in their competitive frame and re-imagine the customer experience. Transformative marketers must understand the implications of this new form of capitalism and envision the new brand stories that it will enable. But more importantly, they need to consider how legacy brands can rewrite or refocus their stories and customer experiences to assure that they do not get left behind.

A Fortune at the Bottom of the Pyramid: The sharing economy is also driving another important trend that is often referred to as the "bottom of the pyramid" effect. This opportunity is represented by the five billion underserved people around the world—about two thirds of the Earth's population. These are people who are seeking innovations to enable them to increase their quality of life with the right value. While traditional, developed markets tend to grow at 1-2% a year, the bottom of the pyramid market is growing 8-9% a year and this represents an enormous opportunity for the future.

"When the poor at the bottom of the pyramid are treated as consumers, they can reap the benefits of respect, choice, and self-esteem and have an opportunity to climb out of the poverty trap."
—C.K. Prahalad, *The Fortune at the Bottom of the Pyramid*

For marketers, facing increasing demands to "do more with less", the bottom of the pyramid could represent a fortune in brand growth potential. "Growing elsewhere" will become increasingly important over the next decade and marketers must be able to adapt their stories, strategies and systems to enter emerging and frontier marketers. However, upon entering these new markets, marketers will encounter an environment that is every bit as complex, if not more so, than developed countries.

Product choices and communication channels are exploding as is the potential of marketing automation platforms. Consumer empowerment is on the rise. Cracking the code on emerging markets and connecting with consumers requires a transformational approach to the overall customer experience. The focus of which should be telling your brand story in a way that makes them the hero. A compelling brand story engages and delights consumers; it makes them want to learn more, want to participate, and want to advocate on a brand's behalf.

The Mastery of the Internet of Things (IoT): By 2020, it is expected that there will be 26 billion devices on the Internet of Things. Broadly defined as the interconnectivity of our digital devices, IoT provides powerful opportunities for marketers to listen, observe and respond to the needs of their target customers with the right message, at the right time, on the right device.

Studies on the IoT have revealed an interesting transformation in the priorities of customers. Led by Millennials, people now want a personalized digital experience. The interconnection of a wide variety of devices redefines the competitive landscape, by enabling marketers to completely personalize customer experiences. This amazing new world of always on, always connected devices will challenge marketing to deliver "real-time relevance" to their customers.

IoT will enable marketers to create totally different experiences by bridging the digital and physical world. Imagine your refrigerator ordering groceries when supplies are running low or notifying emergency services when your aging parent falls down.

"Any sufficiently advanced technology is indistinguishable from magic."
— Arthur C. Clarke, *Profiles of the Future*

Transformative marketers will be entirely data-driven in their operations. From analyzing customer buying habits across their devices, to delivering authentic messaging and fully contextual offers in real-time, the IoT will drive customer experience innovation and create substantial organic growth opportunities for brands to capture.

The Rise of the Blockchain: Most people equate the Blockchain with Bitcoin— the notorious cryptocurrency that is frequently associated with illegal transactions on the "dark web" and traded by nefarious types hiding out from the regulators of monetary systems around the world. In fact, blockchain is the enabling technology behind Bitcoin and many other forms of cryptocurrency, but it represents far more than that. Simply put, Blockchain is a way to store information and keep track of transactions for anything of value. And that information is stored in a secure, immutable, and decentralized data base that is not governed or owned by any third-party.

> *"The Blockchain is an incorruptible digital ledger of economic transactions that can be programmed to record not just financial transactions but virtually everything of value."*
> —Don Tabscott, *Blockchain Revolution*

It is now clear that Blockchain has enough inherent advantages over more conventional stores of digital value that adoption by much of the world is only a matter of time. For marketers, this means the Blockchain is not a question of 'if' it is a question of 'when' their data will be stored in this fashion. Understanding the implications will be critical to success. Everything from the storage of customer transaction data on the cloud, to digital identity of prospects and customer smart contracts for media buying can be enabled through Blockchain technologies. Transformative marketers are already thinking about how their strategies and systems will be impacted and taking steps to learn through experiment with the Blockchain.

Netflix must change, again

In late 2017, Disney surprised the home entertainment industry when it announced that it was launching a digital streaming service for ESPN sports programming and another one dedicated to Disney entertainment. Simultaneously, Disney CEO Bob Iger announced that the media giant would end its lucrative licensing deal with Netflix—shifting distribution of Disney Animation, Pixar films and all its TV shows to its own streaming platform. And just like that, the Mouse declared war on Netflix. No doubt, Reed Hastings and the team at Netflix are gearing up to transform once again and deliver the best home video viewing experience for its customers. I wouldn't underestimate them.

Chapter 2

Transforming Marketing, One Marketer at a Time

Mike Ziegler knew that he faced an uphill battle when he signed on at Ameritox as the SVP of Marketing and Sales in June 2013. But having seen his fair share of hazardous duty as an officer in the Marines, he knew he was up to the task. Ameritox had established itself as a leading brand in pain medication monitoring and urine drug testing services. Their toxicology expertise and accredited laboratory services were highly respected by physicians and health insurance payers. However, at the time, the overall drug testing industry was under intense regulatory scrutiny due to the unscrupulous practices of one of Ameritox's largest competitors, Millennium.

The Department of Justice alleged that Millennium had violated the False Claims Act for billing Medicare, Medicaid and other federal health care programs for medically unnecessary urine drug and genetic testing. The DOJ also alleged that Millennium had given kickbacks to physicians who agreed to refer their expensive laboratory testing business.

Even though Ameritox was not implicated in of any of these violations, the Millennium story was tarnishing all of the players in the industry, lowering the level of reimbursements and eroding overall sales and profitability. Needless to say, Ziegler had to quickly find a way to change the dialog, reposition the Ameritox story and transform marketing and sales operations to deliver growth.

To complicate matters further, Ameritox leadership had committed to achieve aggressive growth plans. They were in the process of launching a new behavioral health division that would focus on the untapped market of helping psychiatrists monitor patients on anti-depressants and antipsychotic drugs. In addition, Ameritox had recently acquired PRIUM, a business specializing in helping companies resolve workers compensation claims, monitoring employee adherence to pain medication prescriptions and getting them back to work as soon as possible. Mike realized that the current messaging for the three brands was complex, poorly focused, and didn't differentiate the company from its competitors. Furthermore, he inherited organizational changes that had created issues with operational efficiencies and gaps in current sales and marketing processes.

Mike kicked off a thorough discovery process—conducting multiple executive workshops and market interviews with the goal of gathering the right information in order to form the foundation of a new and innovative destination for the Ameritox branded lines of business. According to Ziegler, one of the keys to Ameritox's success was "identifying *why* we do what we do as a company." He identified this as a foundational step to drive transformation across the entire organization. He also noted that "it's crucial to establish the ***core values and purpose*** of the company and always put the voice of the customer at the center of the brand's offering and messaging."

Ziegler and his team led the development of brand stories for each of the branded lines of businesses—being certain to illuminate the "why" and reveal clear points of difference and preference drivers focused on making the customer the hero. Even though they offered similar drug and genetic testing protocols, each brand had a different target customer. So, they were required to develop segmentation, targeting, channel and messaging strategies that aligned with the different targets buyers and their unique buyer journeys. They also completed a comprehensive audit of the marketing people, processes, and platforms to ensure they had the right systems in place to activate the brand stories and execute the corresponding go-to-market strategies.

"To transform the company, not just the sales and marketing department, we had to develop a simple and clear message to everyone across the organization as well as those who were communicating with our customers."
— Mike Ziegler, SVP Marketing and Sales, Ameritox

Under Ziegler's leadership, Ameritox was completely transformed with three branded business lines on the path to profitability in the midst of challenging industry headwinds. His restructuring of the Ameritox marketing organization alone resulted in a 25% reduction in staff, marketing spend savings of more than 12% and increased efficiencies across the board. They successfully launched the new behavioral health services division—now branded as Ingenuity Health. Today it serves community mental health centers across the US. With an astounding 300% growth in sales, Ingenuity became the fastest growing division within Ameritox. PRIUM initiated a strategic selling approach which resulted in a 42% closure rate in targeted accounts and ultimately contributed substantially to the growth of the firm.

Organizations like Ameritox and Netflix, that navigate through industry disruption, transform marketing and generate remarkable results for their business, have one thing in common: strong transformative leadership. By reshaping their story, driving change in their industries, and redefining relationships with their customers, leaders like Mike Ziegler and Reed Hastings build remarkable customer experiences and ultimately transform customers into brand advocates.

Transformative marketers know that success depends on the simplicity, clarity, and alignment of their brand's story, strategy, and systems. Yet, they also understand that big change is difficult to achieve from the "top down"—there must be understanding, alignment, and commitment across the organization.

According to executive search firm Korn Ferry, a transformative Chief Marketing Officer (CMO) is marked by these core competencies:

Creating the new and different: The ability to generate new ideas and breakthroughs requires vision, creativity, and broad interests and knowledge.

Focusing on action and outcomes: Transformative CMOs must possess the potent combination of attacking everything with energy—while also keeping an eye on the bottom line.

Inspiring others: Building motivated, high-performing teams—or even moving an entire organization to perform at a higher level—demands a compelling vision, commitment, and superior communication.

These are unquestionably a very different set of core competencies for CMOs than those that might have been enumerated five or ten years ago. The explosion of digital marketing, the empowered customer, and the acceleration of demand for innovation are having a profound impact on customer experiences and expectations.

Driving customer demand no longer relies on the best creative copy or the most entertaining tag-lines. It relies on an analytical, psychological, and perhaps even <u>anthropological</u> understanding of the customer. Transformative marketers can no longer rely on "the way things have always been done" to generate demand. Instead, they must find new, innovative ways to engage their target audience.

As organizations strive to set themselves apart from competitors, marketing has taken on new prominence throughout the business process. We believe that the days of marketing as "brand-builder" and "lead generator" are things of the past. Today, marketing is actually involved with transforming how business is done, and it all starts with the CMO. Another key driver of change: CEOs and corporate boards are scrutinizing marketing activities and budgets with an unprecedented level of analytical intensity.

When you consider the Ameritox story and the leadership of Mike Ziegler and his team, it becomes evident that today's transformative marketer must possess different skills and master unique tools to be successful in the marketplace:

Lean and agile—Transformative marketers must have an understanding of lean and agile principles, and the ability to apply those principles across all systems and strategies. The "always be shipping" approach must be aligned across departments—IT can't run on two-week sprints while Marketing runs on six-month "marathons."

Performance driven—Transformative marketers are results-driven and measure success with KPIs clearly linked to business performance. These marketers have an in-depth understanding of business operations, an analytical approach to problem solving, and the ability to inspire others to action. They build a culture of execution.

Navigate organizational silos - In addition to partnering with the CEO to grow the business, it is the role of transformative marketers to navigate, and in some cases, bring down organizational silos. Transformational marketing initiatives depend on internal alignment of departments, transparency of data, shared information and fully integrated technology stacks to succeed. By quickly identifying and resolving time wasters and bottlenecks, transformative marketers are able to build momentum and drive growth.

Align marketing technology across functions—Transformative marketers use their understanding of cutting-edge Marketing Technology ("MarTech") to assess how it relates to the distinct needs of the organization. MarTech stacks should integrate across departments to create a comprehensive customer view. With over 5,000 vendor solutions in the market today, keeping up with "MarTech" has become a daunting task for any marketer. Does the software align and connect to your existing systems? Does it integrate seamlessly with other business applications? Does it effectively drive customer awareness and engagement?

> *"There is a debate at the moment that we've perhaps tilted the field too much into the swampland of all the mechanics of the technology, that we have lost a bit of that grand vision of what the Story is, to actually guide how we use the technology."*
> — Scott Brinker, VP, Ecosystems at HubSpot

Leaders leading change—In order to lead organizational change, the CMO and the marketing team must be able—not just willing—to work with multiple stakeholders, managers, and employees. From partnering with HR on Employer Branding to working with customer service to QA testing new products/services to compiling and analyzing data, transformative marketers work closely with other departments. They have authentic and frequent interactions with IT, HR, and Finance leaders to ensure the enterprise is creating a seamless and valuable customer experience.

Master customer behavior and journey mapping—Transformative marketers go beyond just crunching the data; they actually talk to the customer and perform customer journey mapping. They ask, "What, if anything, could we do better?" These marketers look beyond the traditional marketing metrics (e.g. brand awareness, familiarity, appeal, etc.) and analyze how the entire enterprise is engaging the customer. By developing a deep understanding of pain points and the overall customer journey, transformative marketers are able to create a simple and compelling brand story that makes customers want to engage.

Own insight to action and drive growth—In marketing circles, it's well known that it's much easier and less complicated to cut costs than it is to drive topline growth. It's not uncommon that the first "strategic" move of a new CMO is to conduct a review of the company's advertising agency.

The stated goal, of course, is to inventory marketing investments, assess performance and audit the agency. However, more often than not, it is just a structured process to drive out costs by introducing competition. So, why don't they start with converting market and customer insights into specific, actionable plays to grow the business? Because driving organic growth is tough.

Transformational marketing requires a little hutzpah and a fair bit of political capital to be expended. Failure will incur a reprimand or worse a pink slip and a trip to the unemployment office. With success, a promotion to the corner office will likely follow.

Transformative marketers are well informed risk-takers. They are the people in the company who get invited to the boardroom, they have a seat at the table and they are often being groomed for leadership. Why? Because they are perceived as owning the insight to action process and they can demonstrate a clear linkage between marketing investments, innovation and organic growth.

Based on our collective experiences helping brands move to the TopRight corner of the market over the past ten years, we've had the privilege of working side-by-side with many transformational marketing "heroes." In concluding this chapter, we thought it would be helpful to share tips from a few of our heroes to help inspire you to transform marketing for your organization:

"In transformational change, the key is to drive simplicity, clarity, and alignment in the story of why this really matters, and what it is specifically that is changing."
— Lidia Frayne, Director of Marketing Operations
at Dell Technologies

"Define the vision — the future-state your company is looking towards — and understand the path to get there. Get everyone focused and aligned around that simple, clear, and compelling Story."
— Scott Klinger, VP Global eCommerce at First Data

"Get the team on board. They are interfacing with customers; they are the ones that can identify the exact problems customers are facing. The team needs to be on board to help drive change and transformation within the organization first to be able to successfully drive change externally."
— Jim Brady, President and CEO of Brady
Trane / Building Clarity

"The most important activity is identifying and creating the Brand Narrative, at the very top level. We have a clear idea of what the Story is for the company, that's been the key touchstone to translate down for other elements were doing as a Marketing Team."
— Scott Barton, Institute for Humane Studies (IHS)
at George Mason University

"My mantra is: always get the right message, at the right time, with the right audience, via the right platform."
— Andrea Koslow, Senior Director, Brand Strategy
at Public Broadcasting Service (PBS)

"Transformational Marketing requires you to walk in the shoes of the customer, experiencing the landscape from the customer's point of view."
— Kelly Chmielewski, Brand Innovator and Founder,
The Possibility Shop

STORY

Chapter 3

Telling a Simple, Yet Remarkable Brand Story

#HR4HR—it couldn't be simpler—tweet using #HR4HR to help our friends in Puerto Rico, Texas and Florida. T-Mobile's Home Runs for Hurricane Recovery effort donated $10,000 for every home run hit during the 2017 Major League Baseball Playoffs and $20,000 per home run during the World Series. To directly engage customers, T-Mobile also agreed to donate $1 for every tweet that includes the #HR4HR hashtag—and doubled-down for the World Series raising the donation to $2 per tweet up to $500,000 on top of the home run total. And the Major League players certainly delivered! They set the all-time record for home runs in a postseason at 103 home runs—resulting in over $2.4M in donations to hurricane relief.

*"We're using our platform on baseball's biggest stage to up our game and
raise awareness for those hit hardest this hurricane season,"*

—John Legere, T-Mobile CEO

The brand also directly engaged MLB players like Evan Longoria, Miguel Sano and Nelson Cruz to tweet to their followers to raise awareness. Players with ties to Florida, Houston and Puerto Rico, communities devastated by hurricanes in 2017, made #HR4HR a part of their personal story and became advocates for T-Mobile in the process.

T-Mobile gets it. Their marketing is all about storytelling—the story of their brand, its purpose and its impact. The advertising images and corresponding copy may be part of it, but the heart of the story is the brand, the service, and the people. If you can stir emotion in customers and they begin to make your story a part of their lives, then you've really created something special.

As customers, we certainly don't know the whole truth about the things we buy, recommend, and use. What we do know, and what we talk about, is our story: our story about why we choose a brand, complain about it, or advocate for it; our story about the origin of our buying decision, the personal utility gained, and the emotional impact of our purchase.

*"Marketing is no longer about the stuff you make, but about the stories
you tell."*

— Seth Godin, Author of All Marketers are Liars

The best brand stories, the most remarkable ones, don't focus on what a company does or the products or services it sells. For example, everyone knows that T-Mobile is a wireless carrier. But that's not their brand story. In fact, they are the "Un-carrier." They are redefining the way people use wireless devices to connect and make a difference in other people's lives. With #HR4HR, T-Mobile rallied people around our national pastime and celebrated every home run with a donation to disaster relief. If you tweeted about it, you could be a hero too. The most effective brand story clearly answers the question, "Why?"—why you do what you do—and why it should matter to the customer.

"Good marketers tell brand stories; great marketers tell them with purpose."

If you have trouble capturing very clearly and directly the essence of why you do what you do and how you do it, then you can bet your customers will, too. It is not unusual for a large company or organization to offer numerous products or services, scattered across markets and targeting different decision-makers with distinct responsibilities, challenges, and desired outcomes. How can you possibly bring simplicity to all of that?

Simplicity in Story

A simple story is not at all about being simplistic. It is the opposite. It's about distilling the true purpose and value of what you offer to customers. Rather than thinking literally about your products, services, and so on, think about what these things represent in the mind of your customer. To achieve simplicity in your story, begin by asking "Why"; and keep asking why until you identify the one thing—the essence—of why you matter.

Think and Feel Like the Customer

Simplicity is important—but only in so far as it relates to your customers. Your "Why" informs how your customers think and feel about you. It defines your position in their minds. Compelling stories resonate when the audience can put itself into the story. Compelling brand stories connect with customers when the customer understands that that story really is about them and their lives. They are not simply being sold to. In other words, the customer is the hero and the story belongs to them, it's about their journey. You are the guide to help them navigate that journey successfully because of what you do for them.

How then do you tell a Brand Story that captures the full intent of your Brand, that gives your customers a reason to listen, a reason to care, a reason to consider, and a reason to buy?

In the early days of advertising, brand storytelling fueled many great campaigns that had the luxury of time to tell a story (on TV, radio, and in print) that spoke to, and resonated with, the audience. In those days, the story was often "long form," complete, and left the readers or viewers with a richer understanding of the brand heritage and the promise of what that brand could mean to them.

With the arrival of the Internet in the mid-1990s, digital storytelling initially followed much of that same pattern (as that is what marketers knew how to do) but in new formats and with new levels of interactivity. Then marketing started to become more of a conversation with the audience than a communication to the audience.

At least that is what we all thought was happening.

However, as our digital lives have become massively cluttered through the explosion of always-on mobile devices and always-on social media, the time for telling our marketing story has shrunk—dramatically. Long-form stories kept shrinking in the online marketing world and there was very little time for reflection or building up to a response. Considering the way digital media is viewed and consumed, and the overwhelming volume of content coming at us every day, what does that shrunken timeframe to tell your story look like?

Telling your Story in 6-seconds

Yes, the timeframe is 6 seconds. You have about a 6-second window for making a connection. Six seconds to give your customers, your audience, a reason to care…a reason to want to learn more. And if that connection is lost in those first few seconds, then it is really lost, and they are most likely not coming back.

This is not an exaggeration.

Think about how you consume information or messages today. If someone has not captured your interest in 6 seconds, you are most likely moving on. In that window of time, the storytelling must be simple, clear, and aligned with your customer's needs and wants.

It must make a bold statement. It must encourage exploration. And it must lead the customer and audience to a question: "How do they do what they say they do?" Or to a pause: "I actually think I need to know more about this." In today's fast-paced environment your Brand Story must:

- Simplify complexity. Your brand assumes the role of a guide or Sherpa who helps them identify their challenges and solve their problems.

- Stir emotion. People buy on emotion and then rationalize their decision with facts.

- Be memorable. Strike a chord that prompts an internal question or reflection. People can more readily relate to a story than fact-laden statements about the wonders of a product.

- Make your customers the hero. Their story (not your brand) is the basis for making the correct decision to use your product or service to fulfill their needs.

And your brand story must do all of this in about 6 seconds. Because that is all the time you will get as they quickly move on to the next site, receive the next message, and experience the next interruption.

Creating a 6-Second Story Isn't Easy

While the length of time you have to tell your brand story has changed, the work required to develop the brand story has not. No matter how short the message, never short-change the depth, complexity, and richness of the story. Creating a 6-second brand story is challenging because it requires a diverse set of scientific skills and an artistic eye to master. In many instances, due to no fault of its own, a company will focus too much attention on either the "science" of gathering actionable insight or the "art" of the story rather than striking the right balance.

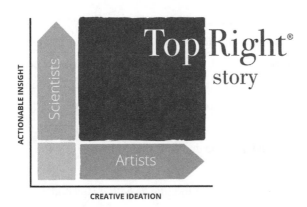

Transformational marketing is a collaborative effort balancing rigorous analysis to drive out actionable audience insights along with the creative ideation and the artistic expression of a storyteller. It's a collaboration. One in which you completely, fully and deeply delve into understanding your target buyer personas and the journey they are on to make a buying decision.

If you understand the customer journey, you can activate your story through an integrated marketing strategy based on what really drives your customers to care, engage, and purchase. This strategy builds your story in a compelling way, resulting in a productive and profitable customer experience where your customers become your advocates.

We've all experienced bad storytelling at some point in our lives: the keynote speaker who reads every word on their PowerPoint slides, the annoying colleague who forgets the punchline to the joke, the pushy salesman who goes off on tangents until he loses his point completely. We roll our eyes, crack our knuckles and just hope that the story comes to a quick and painless ending.

Storytelling, like marketing, is both an art and a science. There are capabilities that are inherently in you as a marketer—like copywriting and creativity—that can be fostered and sharpened, but not necessarily taught. Unfortunately, that art is lost unless you bring a little scientific rigor to your marketing communication planning and execution.

> *"Is your story so compelling that it can transform your customer into a six-second storyteller on your behalf?"*

You'll know you've successfully transformed marketing when your customer not only understands your story but also wants to be a part of it; when your story becomes their story. At that point, your customer's experience transforms from engaging with you in a transaction to becoming part of your community and ultimately an advocate for your brand.

Why? Because they have adopted your story—why you do what you do; what it is that you do; and how you do it—as their own.

> *"Storytelling, like marketing, is both an art and a science."*

As all good marketers know, great copy and engaging creative don't happen by accident. Likewise, great storytelling can't be left to the whims of a "creative genius." You need to inject a level of scientific rigor into the storytelling process that infuses the perspective of your customer into your story. So, there are a few key questions you must answer to make sure you are effectively communicating your story from the customer's point of view:

Why should I care or even listen?

At the core of getting your story right—creating a compelling narrative with purpose and guiding the brand positioning—is the question: "Why do you do what you do?" This sounds easy. As we all know, particularly those of us who have gone through this process, it isn't. It forces you to focus on the difference you actually make for your customers as your guiding principle. For a customer, it requires answering the "so what" question.

Why should a customer care? Why should they listen to your story? Wrestling this question to the ground from the customer point of view requires getting out of the comfort zone of purely marketing a product's features and benefits. This is frequently the default mode for marketers. You must go to a deeper and emotional level of engagement with your customers. You have to distill the company's "why we do what we do?" into a "Why" that captures the customer's imagination.

Unfortunately, most customers have neither the time nor the inclination to figure this out on their own. This is why this question needs to be answered through the simplicity of a great story. For customers, the "Why" must speak to the true impact and purpose that you deliver. This "Why" must resonate with them in such a way that it represents something of which they want to be a part. By simplifying your "Why" and aligning it with your target customers, they will want to learn more about the rest of the story.

"You need to inject a level of scientific rigor into the storytelling process that infuses the perspective of your customer into your story."

What will happen if I engage with your story?

What you do as a company or organization is about what you are *actually doing* to deliver your "Why"; how you are enabling your customers to access and achieve the power and purpose of your "Why", and make it their "Why."

If you have given your customers reasons to care, listen and interact with your brand, you must also convey how that translates to their daily professional and/or personal lives. When your customers engage with you, you must paint a picture of what their life will look like with your product or service, and what would be missing if they choose not to engage with you further. Your customers need to believe in your purpose.

They need to see how that specifically translates to their everyday world. Paraphrasing a line from the movie *Jerry Maguire*: "you complete them" in some way. By filling in that blank with the clarity of what it is you actually do, you can concretely and intentionally transform some aspect of your customers' daily life.

How do I engage with you?

Your customer's journey needs to highlight a clear path to engagement and productive action. What to buy, how to buy, and how to effectively implement and use your products and/or services needs to be specifically told. All of this must flow directly from the "Why" and the "What." Your customers care about your purpose and what that means to them. They can see the impact of how you provide a specific value to them and, as a result, how their life would be different.

The next question is "How" should your customers engage with you? You need to create specific messaging that instructs your customer "How": how they can access your story, your products, and your services, and how to use all of the above to make a difference and impact in their daily lives.

Correctly answering this question requires you to put yourself in the mindset of your customer. You are literally telling them a story of how they should engage with you and then navigating them in a straight line to take a specific action (e.g. buy, renew, review, refer, recommend). If customers have to work too hard to figure this out, it means your story is not working and they will not be engaging with, buying from, or advocating for your brand.

Can I understand your story in 6 seconds?

There has been a fair bit of debate over the past few years about just how much advertising the typical person is exposed to each day. 500 messages?

5,000 messages? 50,000 messages? While the exact numbers are interesting to ponder, no one debates the fact that the total number of messages has been increasing steadily due to the distribution impact of the Internet, the proliferation of "screens", and the pervasiveness of mobile devices in our daily lives.

> *"We've gone from being exposed to about 500 ads a day*
> *back in the 1970s to as many as 5,000 a day today."*
>
> – J Walker Smith, Chief Knowledge Officer,
> Brand and Marketing, Kantar Consulting

The implications? Well, for one, businesses need to do something special to be noticed in this cluttered environment. And secondly, with all of the multi-tasking going on, you better be quick about it!

Here is the simple truth of marketing and communications today: you have roughly six seconds to earn the attention of your prospective customer. A six-second window for making a connection. Six seconds to give your target audience a reason to care and a reason to want to learn more. Furthermore, if that connection is lost in those first few seconds, then it is really lost and they are most likely not coming back.

Does your story, and how your customer experiences that story, make them want to engage with you further—giving you the chance to close a sale?

Does it pass the test of simplicity, clarity, and alignment in six seconds?

Is your brand story so compelling that it can transform your customer into a six-second storyteller on your behalf?

Remember, the point of marketing is not always about closing the sale. Sometimes you are just starting a conversation and inviting your audience to spread that conversation in their own authentic voice of advocacy.

Where are you taking me?

After your customer understands your story, they will care and want to learn more. They will want to engage with you and learn how to buy, and maybe even advocate on your behalf. When your customers embrace your six-second story and why it matters to them and their lives, you are in a conversation with them because they want to be in that conversation.

Where will you take your customers over the long term? At what destination will your brand and the customer arrive together? For your customers to truly understand and activate your brand story in their lives, this is the final and most essential question for your customers to be able to answer.

"What is the destination that I arrive at by engaging with you, buying from you, and advocating for you?"

By embracing a transformational marketing approach, you will tell the story of why you matter to your customers today. You will show them what their journey looks like in the future, and how that journey will change their experience.

You are not the hero of the story. Your customer is the hero. You are merely the guide, the Sherpa, that leads them to a destination which they could not get to on their own. That destination is the culmination of your 6-second Story (the Why, What, and How) pointed directly at a destination to which you are uniquely able to guide them.

Upon arriving at the destination, your customer has made your story their own. They want your help in leading them because they understand the impact of what you are offering them—that the place you will arrive at together could actually be transformative.

"Make the customer the hero of your story."
— Ann Handley, Chief Content Officer, MarketingProfs

So, that's it. Take the time to answer these key questions and you will be on your way to bringing scientific rigor to the art of your story. Your answers to these questions will make a big difference in whether your audience views your story as just another transactional relationship or a story that emotionally connects with their professional or personal journey.

The only story that really matters is the one where your customers want to become part of the story. And for them to do that, they need to understand it and what it means for them, through the lens of simplicity, clarity, and alignment.

Chapter 4

Telling a Nonprofit Brand Story

The man in the Santa costume rings his bell outside a bustling store. As you exit with your shopping bags, tucking your credit card back in your wallet, you pause. The crowd continues moving around you, but you stop to scrounge a few spare coins from your pocket and drop them in the red collection box. The resulting clink doesn't really make you feel good, but it does make you feel slightly less guilty until next December, when you'll do it all again.

The marketing team at German relief organization, Misereor has been "thinking outside the collection box" when it comes to transforming their donor's experience.

Misereor supports people around the world through self-help initiatives. Their story is one that many nonprofits attempt to tell: in the fight against poverty and injustice, even a small donation can have a big impact. However, donations have been on a steady decline for many years. That generic story just doesn't work anymore.

To increase people's willingness to give, the marketing team at Misereor transformed the donation process by developing digital media displays with built-in credit card swiping capabilities. They then installed them in Germany's busiest airports. One display simply reads "Feed them," showing a video image of a loaf of bread from above. Users are asked to make a small, secure donation (only €2) to help end hunger.

When the credit card is swiped, it acts like a knife through the loaf. You know the donation transaction is complete when the slice falls to the counter and a hand reaches out to take it. The message is clear: this donation feeds hungry people, and you helped do that. The effect is a cohesive story that's powerful, personal, and actionable. Doesn't it feel good?

Misereor's "Social Swipe" story engages its audience rather than incites and neatly overcomes barriers to donation in two key ways. First, the mechanism for donation is eye-catching: Cutting through bread to give a slice to a hungry person is a powerful visual representation that shows exactly how your money is helping people. The visual depiction identifies the recipients and direct benefits of aid, making the link between donation and relief much more tangible.

Secondly, the efficiency and ease of the mechanics only add to this campaign's merit. By asking for a credit card donation, rather than cash, the charity overcomes those sheepish looks from potential donors who lack small change. By adapting to this consumer shift, this campaign neatly sidesteps a key stumbling block for many fundraisers.

There are many reasons why the Misereor story works better than passive, interruptive fundraising attempts like collection boxes or people in Santa suits ringing bells. The interactive element is creative and novel, enticing first-time donors and prompting sharing through social media. And the engagement doesn't end after one swipe; participants are given the option to set up recurring donations to Misereor through their bank statements, allowing the charity to retarget a group of donors more likely to be engaged and stay engaged.

At its core, this nonprofit story works because it follows the tenets of transformational marketing: a simple story that inspires, a clear strategy that engages, and a smart system that is aligned to deliver a donor experience worthy of remark.

While other nonprofits were out hiring another Santa Claus, Misereor found a way to break through the clutter and transform the donor experience. Their story, strategy and systems work together seamlessly for a delightful experience that makes us all feel good to do good.

The Result?

At €2 a donation (US$2.37), Misereor was able to collect 1,500 one-off donations in the first month alone at the airport. While that number could suggest that the charity might be wasting time chasing one time donors, Misereor was also able to increase their number of sustaining donors (those who donated three or more times) by 23% through the credit card program.

Breaking Through the Clutter

If you've scrolled through Facebook lately, you've likely seen that a lot of your good friends have become amateur philanthropists. Facebook's new fundraising feature, a huge improvement on their "causes" product, has created a flurry of nonprofit stories entering our lives. And though the new platform still has infrastructure issues, you can't help but feel optimistic at how Facebook has made it so easy to give. But with this ease comes proliferation. Facebook fundraising has the potential to be a powerful tool for nonprofits, but how do we sift through the noise?

Our digital lives have become so cluttered through the explosion of "always on" culture—always on mobile devices and always on social media. These crowdfunding tools, amplified by social media's ability to distribute information, have only made it more and more difficult for nonprofits to get noticed amidst the noise.

On average, your brand story has to get its message across in a way that's clear, compelling, actionable and aligned in about 6 seconds. So how do you get through the clutter to tell your story?

Here are a few tips for creating an effective nonprofit brand story that will give people a reason to care, a reason to give and ultimately a reason to advocate on your behalf.

Keep it Simple

You only have 6 seconds, remember? So, you need to grab the viewer's attention as quickly as possible with a simple and clear brand story that spells out your mission. If you can convince them to stay to listen, there's a greater chance they'll want to learn more and join in your story. Make your story simple and easily digestible.

Make it Personal

People are more likely to engage with your nonprofit if you frame the interaction around real stories from real people. If your nonprofit is making a difference in people's lives, capture those stories and find ways to talk about what you do within the context of their personal journeys.

Appeal to Emotion

Your Story needs to inspire the viewer to identify with your cause and motivate them to engage with your organization. To do that, you need to create powerful stories that engage with their emotions. The goal is not to manipulate the consumer or persuade them into thinking a certain way; it's to make them *feel* something.

Make it Memorable

Make that connection. Make the user engage, remember you, and want to share your story. People can more readily relate to a story than fact-laden statements, so aim to make the message a memorable one. Remember that memorable doesn't necessarily mean perfect. Find what's unique about your organization and let that influence your brand story.

Have a Clear, Aligned Objective

With such a small timeframe to make an impression, your words have to work really hard. There's no room for confusion, so clarity of language and objectives is key. What is the most important thing to convey to your potential donors? Make sure your story is aligned with this objective.

Make it Actionable

Six seconds. That's all the time you have to get someone to care. And if the customer actually listens, what do they do next? It's important to provide a call-to-action so the consumer doesn't have to search in order to act. Make it something they want to do and can do as easily as possible.

You have a 6-second window to make a connection with prospective donors, volunteers and program participants. Just 6 seconds to give people a reason to care, listen, engage and give. We know it's difficult to achieve all of that, especially in such a small window of time, but with a simple, clear and aligned brand story, your nonprofit can break through the noise.

Striking the Right Balance between Marketing and Fundraising

Most nonprofit organizations (NPOs) have separate and distinct marketing and development functions. Historically, this division of critical activities has been done for good reason—to bring specific focus on building awareness for the mission and driving fundraising. However, there is significant opportunity in closer collaboration.

Not only are these two functional areas aligned in service to the key audiences and supporters of the organization, they both are employing similar tactics to understand the needs and motivations of those audiences. At best, disjointed insights efforts are costly, and at worst, they work at cross-purposes through confused messaging in the marketplace.

Collaborating on insights and market data should be the rule, but instead, it's rare. Alignment of marketing and fundraising is critical to a nonprofit's success in effectively engaging donors and driving growth. Creating a compelling donor experience relies heavily on your NPO's ability to align goals, audience insights, and your compelling, six-second story across marketing and development departments.

> *"We are more alike, my friends, than we are unalike."*
>
> — Maya Angelou

Maya Angelou may not have been referring specifically to nonprofit marketing and development teams but her words hold true nonetheless — the two functions are far more alike than different, especially now that each function engages the same audience through digital and social channels.

Development is a distinct function from marketing in many nonprofits, similar to how sales and marketing teams *used* to be in the corporate world. Just as digital disruption inspired the alignment of sales and marketing in for-profits, nonprofit marketing and development teams must follow suit.

The alignment of marketing and development operations is a significant opportunity to provide higher returns, more value to supporters, and a stronger position in the marketplace. To get started, we have identified 5 actionable steps that can make a big impact on your alignment efforts:

1. **Suggest identifying areas of collaboration in the next staff meeting**
   Regardless of your title, department, or longevity in the organization, you can get this conversation started. Best case is that legacy distrust or long-held hesitations are brought forward and discussed. The worst-case scenario is that the idea gets shot down unilaterally, and you learn something about your organization.

2. **Understand the goals and objectives of both marketing and development teams**
   Current overlap and shared purpose is a great place to start to formalize new levels of collaboration. By aligning your organizational goals and insights across your marketing and development teams you can craft a simple and clear brand story that will connect consistently and authentically with your target audience.

5 MUTUAL GOALS & FUNCTIONAL EFFORTS
FOR MARKETING & FUNDRAISING

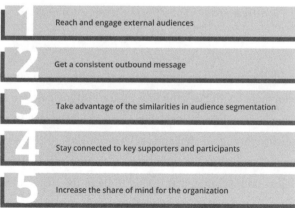

1. Reach and engage external audiences

2. Get a consistent outbound message

3. Take advantage of the similarities in audience segmentation

4. Stay connected to key supporters and participants

5. Increase the share of mind for the organization

3. **Start exchanging key audience survey information across departments**
   Call on your counterparts in other departments who are also doing surveys of key audiences. Share insights, align feedback, and determine potential overlap for future efforts. If marketing serves fundraising activities, then it is also true that the development team must be willing to be served. Collaboration is key—and it starts with recognizing the mutual goals.

4. **Identify a collaboration opportunity to prove your point**
   Start small with a collaborative project to demonstrate the power of shared inputs and talent. Celebrate small wins as proof of concept for larger projects.

5. **Embrace creative tension to drive change**
   Embrace the opportunity to overcome organizational inertia and build an audience insights function that can become a shared services operation for the entire organization. The gap between where you want to go and where you are is also a source of energy. If there were no gap, there would be no need for any action to change. Generating this kind of "creative tension" requires clarity about your desired brand destination and full organizational alignment on the "truth about today."

Overcoming the challenges of misalignment between marketing and development functions allows you to get the most out of your scarce resources. This enables your nonprofit to tell a unified brand story that gives prospective donors, volunteers and program participants a reason to care, a reason to learn, and a reason to give and advocate for your cause.

Chapter 5
Telling a Story to Win Talent

Asurion, LLC is a privately held company based in Nashville, Tennessee that provides mobile protection insurance and technology warranty support services. Their brand story is about "supporting the tech that keeps you connected." They enable people across the globe to balance their interdependency between life and technology. Today, they assure that over 300 million customer devices and appliances stay online and on the job keeping people optimally productive.

In order to fulfill their brand promise, Asurion relies heavily on attracting and retaining the brightest talent to serve their customers. However, as a "white-label" protection company standing behind big brands like Apple, Samsung and Verizon, Asurion struggles to be recognized by top talent as an employer of choice. In short, they're one of the biggest and most advanced technology companies that you've never heard of.

In the technology sector, the war for talent is real. We're experiencing one of the toughest talent shortages in a long time. The amount of "time to hire" is in a seemingly never-ending rise and 68% of HR managers say they're having trouble filling positions. Hiring managers compete fiercely for the right candidates within a very limited talent pool.

Not surprisingly, top talent is drawn to the magnetic stories of big brands like Google, Facebook and Microsoft. These brands promise their employees cutting-edge technical work, rapid career advancement, breakthrough innovation opportunities and cushy benefits packages. Tech recruiting and retention has become a complex and dynamic battlefield that the human resources team at Asurion knows all too well.

So, in 2016, the talent acquisition and retention teams at Asurion realized they needed to change the rules of engagement if they were going to win their fair share of top talent. They needed a clear and authentic story about why a technology candidate should join and why current high-performing employees should stay at Asurion for their career.

David Marks was tapped by Asurion leadership to develop a compelling employer brand story to stand out from the 'sea of sameness' and differentiate the company from competing employers in the markets they serve. And then, effectively communicate that story to reach the high-quality talent they seek and assure that the employee experience is fully aligned and consistent with the promise of the story.

David and his team conducted in-depth interviews with select employees and candidates to understand the various factors that influence their decision to join and/or stay with Asurion. They identified specific benefit corridors via in-depth interviews and verified their hypotheses through quantitative research. Data from this exercise was transformed into actionable insights through an analytic methodology to identify not only what's important to employees and candidates, but also what ultimately drives their behavior to join and/or stay at Asurion.

Asurion surveyed over 750 individuals currently working or seeking employment within the technology sector in three specific functional roles: Technology Implementation, Research and Development, and Customer Service and Support. Below is a quick overview of the findings:

Money talks in a competitive job market

Unsurprisingly, high compensation is top of mind and ranks as the most important motivator for the majority of respondents for their job. Someone has to pay the bills!

Motivations differ across roles

When you dive into specific job functions, the data revealed that although the majority of respondents indicated they are "Progressors" (i.e. highly focused on career progression), their job motivations differ significantly.

Specifically, for a Technology implementation role, respondents ranked job security as the strongest motivator in their daily work. While for R&D and Customer Service and Support roles, respondents ranked opportunities for advancement as their top motivation.

For the R&D role, the respondents were much more likely to "do their homework" before they jump into career-related decisions. Also, they desire to work for and stay with an organization that fosters career advancement and provides intellectually challenging opportunities.

In the Customer Service and Support role, most people align with the persona of "Influencers"—they are persuasive individuals with positive attitudes. They're typically excellent at steering customers to resolution. The data shows that they desire to join and stay with an organization that values employee contributions and invests in their growth and development.

For the Progressors in the Technology Implementation role, most are "Visionaries"—they think big picture and conceptualize ideas to motivate others to action. They are attracted to join and stay with an organization that is forward-thinking and where they can make a difference.

In the face of the currently challenging job market, firms struggling with communicating consistent and authentic messaging that resonates with the talent they seek will continue to lose in the war for the best talent.

The team used these new insights and many more to develop a simple, yet compelling, employer brand story. A framework was created to tailor the story to different target roles and different touchpoints in the employee's journey to make sure that messaging was authentic and relevant to the audience.

The early results have been impressive, Asurion generated actionable insights into what drives candidates to join and employees to stay with a technology company like Asurion including things like:

- Career-enhancing guidance and growth opportunities for people

- Passionate leaders who value team success and create a rewarding and supportive work environment

- Flexibility in time and location for people to do their work and achieve peak productivity and performance

- Recognition of accomplishments and contributions through competitive compensation

- An environment that champions strong social awareness and ethical standards

- An environment where leaders authentically embody and promote the organizational core values

- An environment that inspires a sense of pride in the work people do and the impact they can make

Asurion simplified and clarified their employer brand story and aligned it with specific role descriptions to assure that the messaging differentiates Asurion and reinforces the desired behaviors at every step of the employee journey.

Employer Brand Story

If you are a tenacious professional wanting to push yourself, test your potential and exceed your limits, Asurion is the right employment choice as a leading technology company that offers career enhancing experiences where there are opportunities to learn, grow and help people get more out of their connected life.

If the challenges faced by Asurion sound familiar to you, you're not alone. If you've been trying to build your staff as a recruiter, hiring manager, business owner, or in an HR leadership position, you've most likely had some trouble. Let's be frank… a lot of trouble.

One of the keys to great employer branding is being authentic by presenting a true image of the company culture and making sure it's aligned with the brand's story. If you think this happens without a ruthlessly consistent effort remember—your employer brand is already being created on social media by employees and people who have interacted with your hiring process. If you doubt that, take a few minutes right now and check out your company on Glassdoor.com.

People are already talking about your company, so you have to ask yourself whether or not you want a voice in the creation of your employer brand story. What do you do when a prospective job candidate or former employee leaves a negative review of your business?

Here are a few tips to help you respond to poor online reviews from prospective job candidates and former employees:

- Respond promptly

- Be calm

- Ensure you "hear" their complaints

- Correct inaccuracies stated in the review

- Emphasize your strengths

- Write like a "real person" not a corporation

- Be consistent

- Remember future candidates will see this

- Be proactive

You can use negative feedback to enhance your HR and recruiting process as well as understand what you candidates are seeking. In this highly competitive labor market, the power of an effective employer brand cannot be underestimated as it helps to effectively communicate key benefits that will attract qualified candidates and retain current employees.

LinkedIn's Global Recruiting Trends Report uncovered key trends worldwide that organizations should focus on for 2016. At the top of that list was employer branding — and for good reason. It is a key component to attracting new talent and retaining current rock stars. Considering that 66 percent of companies surveyed report having trouble finding the right talent and 65 percent admitting this impacts their bottom line (ADP), now is the time to invest in your employer brand.

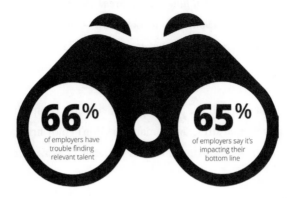

The employer brand is essentially how a company is seen through the eyes of potential candidates and employees.

Your employer brand is not simply a company logo or career page. Instead, it is the emotional reaction people have to the idea of working for your company.

Authenticity Leads to Alignment

Authentic employer branding accurately reflects a company's culture and is clearly aligned with the brand story, strategy, and systems. Finding candidates that align with the company is one of the main benefits of investing in a strong employer brand.

By clearly communicating the employer brand, both the candidate and company can equally assess the culture fit. Not only will this result in attracting the best talent out there, but it will also result in hires that perform better on the job.

GE's "What's the Matter with Owen?" campaign is designed to reintroduce the 123-year-old company as a place that young technology talent can do meaningful work. In the commercials, a newly hired programmer struggles to explain the importance of his role to friends and family who are far more impressed with the guy working on the "Zazzies" app.

"As a brand, we are constantly thinking about what's new and next for the world with our technology, and to mirror that it in our marketing and the way we tell our story. It is representative of how we think as a company—it's

in our DNA.... This idea of how can we break this notion of 'impossible.' It is kind of a mission everyone who works at GE — particularly our scientists and engineers — wakes up and thinks about."

— Linda Boff, GE CMO

New hires that don't fill the position effectively cost companies time, money, and unnecessary mental stress. Most managers don't enjoy firing employees; and interviewing candidates is taxing and takes valuable focus away from growing the bottom-line.

Tap into your Employees

When it comes to finding talent, employees are valuable brand advocates. Not only does it takes a shorter length of time to hire a qualified candidate via employee referral, but referred employees also have a longer tenure.

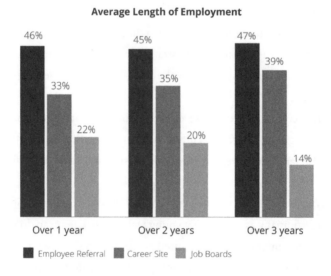

Average Length of Employment

Employee referrals typically mean that the candidate has been pre-screened and identified as a good culture fit. One employer brand that is on-point is MailChimp, an marketing automation company based in Atlanta.

"I only hire weirdos, basically, and I just let them fail all the time. It just makes perfect sense to me."

—Ben Chestnut, MailChimp CEO

By investing in your current employees and empowering them to do work that matters to them, you foster a loyal and dynamic team. Every MailChimp employee who has posted reviews on Glassdoor said they would recommend the company to a friend, and 100% approve of the CEO.

"We provide an environment that allows for, and encourages, acting on spontaneous creativity."

—Dan Kurzius, MailChimp co-founder

To understand the general perception of your employer brand, external research can be conducted through applicant surveys, Internet searches, or social media. A telltale sign your employer brand needs work is a lack of employee referrals.

Simply stated, if the employees don't feel good about the place, they're not going to subject to their friends to the environment. What kind of friend does that?

Your employer brand has a great impact on the recruitment of potential candidates and retention and engagement of current employees, both of which are keystones to sustainable growth. It's your responsibility to understand the current perception of candidates and clearly communicate your story.

Behind the Scenes on Social Media

A seemingly obvious channel in which to tell that story is social media. According to a recent Universum Global study, in the next 5 years there will be a 70 percent increase in the use of social media for promoting employer brand.

Zappos is an excellent example of how to do employer branding right on social media. The company's Instagram page, InsideZappos, gives a real inside look into what it is like working for the company. By sharing pictures, blogs, and videos through the company's social media channels, Zappos is able to help positively shape its employer brand.

You've also got to consider the way the competition approaches the same candidates. Your brand story involves more than just what you say about your company—it also involves positioning the competition so that the debate is on your terms. Control the dialogue, control the message, and you control the competition—don't let them go putting ideas into your candidates' heads!

Finally, keep in mind that preference is perishable. Just because someone has an affinity for your brand story today doesn't mean they're going to hang around and wait for you to make an offer. If you don't reevaluate your brand story in the marketplace to keep up with employee attitudes, you're likely to find yourself without any suitors at all.

Every organization's reputation as an employer — whether it's positive, negative or "meh" — will become increasingly important to attracting and retaining the best and brightest minds. Telling a simple, clear and fully aligned employer brand story will move your company to the TopRight corner of the markets where you compete.

Chapter 6

Telling a Story in Emerging Markets

The Weber-Stephen company was facing what seemed to be an incredibly difficult task: successfully launching their classic outdoor barbecue grills in India. The iconic "Weber Kettle" had no local brand awareness and a "backyard barbecue" culture was non-existent in the country.

Enter Sivakumar ("Siva") Kandaswamy, the man who Weber tapped to take on this challenge. Siva knew that Weber's successful market entry in India would depend largely on creating demand for its brand while simultaneously creating an entirely new category for outdoor cooking. The cultural differences in India were one of the first obstacles he faced. For example, the typical Indian male does not cook, most Indians believe that barbecue means non-vegetarian food, and "do-it-yourself" outdoor cooking is uncommon. Siva also faced challenges like highly fragmented distribution channels, limited space available at retail, language diversity (23 official languages!), and aggressive price competition from many Chinese and local manufacturers. Significant headwinds for a US-based barbecue grill company!

Siva recognized the solution would require building the category and the brand from the ground-up in India. With no data available on the current sales or consumer behavior in the category, he gathered consumer insights through primary research. Insights gave Weber a springboard for launching a differentiated Brand Story in India. He followed that up by developing a multi-channel strategic playbook. This helped him to articulate the plays he would need to run on the ground with dealers and distributors across the country to get the Weber Story in front of the target audience. Finally, he put the Systems (people, process, and technology) in place to execute the Strategy with ruthless consistency and enable Weber to scale up across the country.

Thanks to Weber, a backyard grilling culture has taken hold in India. Indian families enjoy outdoor grilling and Weber delivers additional benefits by providing consumers with tips, tools, and localized recipes. Weber has been able to "grow elsewhere" by tapping into one of the world's largest markets and expanding their global brand footprint in the process.

Rapid economic growth in countries such as India is giving its consumers new spending power and making them extremely attractive targets for brand marketers around the world. India's economy is one of the fastest expanding in the world, with a rapidly growing consumer class. Representing the world's second biggest population, with 440mn millennials and 390mn Gen Z teens and children, the absolute size of its youth population paves the way for India's consumer story to be one of the world's most compelling in the next 20 years. India's economic liberalization began in the early 1990s and has accelerated ever since.

It seems that every year, new sectors of the economy are opening for foreign direct investment. For example, the Indian Government recently decided to encourage foreign investment in the multi-brand retail sector. This will create huge opportunities for companies involved in agriculture, consumer goods, retail, transportation, and infrastructure in the cold chain logistics sector.

However, business leaders seeking to enter emerging markets like India are encountering a marketing environment that is every bit as complex, if not more so, than developed countries. Product choices and communication channels are exploding as is the potential of marketing automation platforms. Consumer empowerment is on the rise. Envisioning consumer behavior in these markets as a progression through a funnel is inaccurate. It's more of a spiral with multiple feedback loops and numerous touch points where marketers can influence (or frustrate) the consumer on their buying journey.

As in developed markets, digital media and marketing automation are unleashing the possibility of deeper audience engagement at each phase of the journey. But there are some important differences in the characteristics of emerging-market consumers. They generally don't have the same level of experience with brands and product categories as their developed-market counterparts do. Keep in mind that many consumers in these markets are still looking to buy their first car, first television, or first package of diapers.

Marketers in North America are under tremendous pressure to find ways to "grow elsewhere" and to deliver successful emerging market penetration plans and associated marketing strategies. Having worked with numerous brands over the past ten years, we have witnessed many successes… but also multiple failures. Here are the eight most common mistakes that marketers make when trying to build a brand and launch in Emerging Markets:

8 COMMON MISTAKES
WHEN TRYING TO 'GROW ELSEWHERE'

1 Moving too slowly	2 Moving too quickly
3 Thinking that 'Amazon' is a strategy	4 Overinvesting in local customers
5 Telling an irrelevant brand story	6 Being overconfident about Strategy & Systems
7 Underestimating the role of local stakeholders	8 Failing to embrace transformational marketing

1. **Moving too slowly:** Brands that hesitate to get into emerging markets stand to lose out on the best opportunities and concede significant market share. Recovering from loss of market share and playing "catch up" is an expensive proposition and the loss may prove irreversible.

   For example, Starbucks late entry in India in 2012 has allowed the Indian coffee chain Café Coffee Day to beat Starbucks at its own game. Café Coffee Day now has more than 1500 locations in India, while Starbucks has only 75 locations.

2. **Moving too quickly:** Chasing "bright shiny objects" and reacting to opportunities while being unaware of different capabilities needed to operate in unfamiliar markets leaves managers scrambling to deliver on customer expectations and incurring heavy expenses to close the marketing capability gap. These "blind spots" erode profitability, and the lack of success makes the company vulnerable to valuation penalties by investors, as well as opening the door for aggressive competitors to enter the market and steal share.

   Electrolux, the appliances and consumer durables brand, entered in India in a big way in 1995. Its strategy was to grow quickly through acquisitions (e.g. Eureka, Forbes, and Delineator) and then integrate the units into Electrolux India. Overnight, it became an extensive "house of brands." Since the acquired companies varied widely in their culture and practices, Electrolux stumbled and lost its way in the market. Conflicting brand stories and inconsistent go-to-market strategies made many appliance retailers confused and uninterested in carrying their products.

3. **Thinking that "Amazon" is a Strategy for Emerging Markets:** Just because you have customers who are buying your products through e-Commerce does not mean that you have cracked an emerging market. e-Commerce plays a critical role in evaluating and conditioning a market for a new entry Strategy. However, e-Commerce is not a substitute for having a Brand Story connecting emotionally with your target audience at a local level. You need a multi-channel Strategy that gets your Story in front of the right audiences and gives them a reason to listen, a reason to

care, a reason to engage and a reason to buy. Also needed are the right Systems to scale and flawlessly execute your Strategy.

Poor logistics systems and infrastructure compared to other developed countries can create challenges for a strategy predominantly focused on e-commerce, especially in countries where much of the population lives in remote rural areas. Retailers prefer commercial airfreight for delivery, which increases costs. Also, consumers in some countries are not accustomed to making purchases with credit cards. When the local custom is to pay in cash, brand stories that are reliant on e-commerce strategies and systems will likely fail.

4. **Overinvesting in local customers**: Spending too much on customer-centric activities prevents brands from understanding the needs of other valuable stakeholders: government agencies, suppliers, distributors, and important family relations in family-owned businesses. By working in a vacuum, brands pay a high price for unforeseen gaps in the local industry and for poorly understood market and distribution dynamics.

   Vodafone learned this lesson the hard way. They have been locked in a $2.2 billion tax dispute with the Indian government who claims that Vodafone owes the bill for acquiring an Indian subsidiary in 2007. The mobile phone company won a court battle to overturn the ruling. But in response, the previous congress-led government promptly enacted new legislation allowing the firm to be taxed retrospectively. The lack of transparency has been criticized by foreign firms, but government officials asserts that Westerners are often overly concerned with winning customers, but ignore the local rules and the legal system.

5. **Telling an irrelevant brand story for the local market or not telling brand story:** Being relevant to a market means that a brand is cognizant of and willing to address the needs and interests of a wide range of local stakeholders. The Brand Story must center on making the customer and the local stakeholders the hero—rather than making the brand the hero. Marketers with narrow views of how to achieve success (i.e. focusing almost exclusively on short-term financial or market share gains, rather

than, say, helping train local suppliers) fail to become integrated contributors that help elevate the standard of the local industry. Consequently, they do not prosper as well as firms that show they are willing to stay the course during the ups and downs of the local economy.

Group SEB, the French home appliances maker, has relaunched Tefal durable products around a brand story to help Indian consumers "get the best out of everyday." This story positions Tefal products as the 'hero'—assuring consumers that by using the product it will make the Indian home a better place. Group SEB is still trying to crack the market, largely because the story is unclear on how Tefal delivers value, lacks relevance for most Indian homemakers, and fails to position the consumer as the hero.

6. **Being overconfident about Strategy and Systems:** Brands assume that the capabilities that served them well in developed markets are sufficient to succeed in emerging markets. Overconfidence results in underinvestment in mission critical local capabilities and keeps executives from objectively analyzing how well prepared their businesses are to meet the challenges of fast changing emerging economies.

The initial foray of consumer packaged goods company Kellogg's into the Indian market in 1994 was a failure. Although today, the company is doing well in terms of both market share and sales growth. Following their launch, initial sales seemed promising but consumers were just buying the product as a one-off novelty and not repeating the purchase. Kellogg's was overconfident and overlooked many critical cultural insights that would explain why the market wasn't ready for the breakfast cereals offered. Also, the premium pricing strategy was misaligned and too high to be considered as a regular grocery purchase for shoppers, explaining the lack of repeat sales.

7. **Underestimating the role of local stakeholders and governmental organizations:** Governments can and do impose hard terms and conditions on western companies. Successful brands have learned to meet opposing views half way, thus opening the path to long-term success. They understand that insensitivity toward the needs of local governments and local

leaders may result in costly penalties, delays, excessive red tape, and may even challenge business continuity.

Nestlé spent three decades building a beloved noodle brand Maggi in India. Then, the world's biggest food and beverage company stumbled into a public relations debacle that cost it half a billion dollars. Management was blinded by pride and approached regulators with arrogance. Nestle acknowledged that they didn't manage the Maggi crisis communications well.

8. **Failing to embrace a Transformational Marketing approach:** Most business leaders dislike change. They prefer the status quo and view changes to existing marketing and operations tactics as costly distractions when entering a new market. They may also fear losing influence, putting their personal career ambitions at risk and maybe missing out on an upcoming promotion.

Successful brands avoid the gravitational pull from "better sameness" and strike a balance between transformational activities by embracing a holistic perspective on Brand Story, Strategy and Systems: creating a "3S Playbook" to assess, reconfigure, develop, and evolve their marketing to succeed in emerging markets.

World Kitchen's launched into the Indian homewares market in partnership with local market leader TTK Prestige ended after less than two years. Lack of Indian market vision, underestimation of the enduring preference for metal homewares, and failure to embrace a transformational marketing approach led to disappointing sales for the World Kitchen's premium dishware brand: Corelle.

It's easy to make mistakes. But as we learned in the Weber backyard barbecue story, there is a step-by-step process that you can follow to increase your likelihood of emerging market success. You must develop a practical, systematic market entry playbook to help reduce risks, maximize ROI, compete efficiently, and win in emerging markets.

Cracking into emerging markets and connecting with consumers requires a transformational approach to the overall customer experience and, more importantly, telling your brand story in a way that makes them the hero. A compelling brand story engages and delights consumers; it makes them want to learn more, want to participate, and want to advocate on a brand's behalf.

Chapter 7

Crafting Your Personal Brand Story

Imagine tasting a freshly baked brownie by Martha Stewart. Now, imagine Snoop Dogg offering you a freshly baked brownie.

What comes to mind when you think of each one?

Chances are that each scenario represents different things in not only your mind but that of others too.

This is the power of a personal brand.

Who can forget the 2016 U.S. presidential election battle between Hillary Clinton and Donald Trump? Regardless of your political perspective, both candidates embody extremely distinct personal brands. What those brands represent is a different topic, but there's little question that their personal brands played an enormous role in their campaigns and the outcome of the election. You could even argue that their personal brands were bigger than themselves.

Here's the newsflash: you don't have to be famous in order to have a personal brand. Everyone, including you, already has one. No matter who you are, building a compelling personal brand is critical. Not only is a personal brand extraordinarily powerful, but it exists whether you plan for it or not, so why not make it very deliberate?

It must give people a reason to care, a reason to pick you, and a reason to stay. There is a huge difference between whether your audience views your personal brand as just another transactional relationship or a brand that emotionally connects with them.

When people think of you, what comes to mind? What do you stand for? What do you stand against? Is that what you'd like them to think? Is it consistently represented through everyone who engages with you?

In the same way that corporate brands are built, individuals can build their own personal brands. All great brands personify simplicity, clarity, and alignment.

In his book *Brand Called You*, Tom Peters famously pointed out, "We are all CEOs of our own companies: Me Inc." When his book was published in 1997, "mass media" meant traditional broadcast media that were centrally controlled and managed by powerful corporations. The average consumer had little—if any—access to get their message into the market.

> *"To be in business today, our most important job is to be head marketer for the brand called You."*
>
> — Tom Peters

Fast forward to today when digital media dominates. Applications like Instagram, Facebook, LinkedIn, SnapChat, Twitter, and YouTube have revolutionized the media landscape. "Mass media" has taken on an entirely new meaning as the masses control much of the dialog about brands and their reputations in the marketplace. For your personal brand, this shift represents a tremendous opportunity, but also creates challenges that require you to proactively manage your brand and reputation.

Creating a compelling personal brand can be challenging. It requires honesty, authenticity, discipline, and an artistic eye. That said, there are a few common ingredients and guidelines to help you build a compelling personal brand:

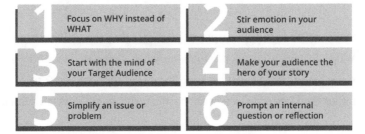

GUIDELINES TO BUILD
A COMPELLING **PERSONAL BRAND**

1. Focus on WHY instead of WHAT
2. Stir emotion in your audience
3. Start with the mind of your Target Audience
4. Make your audience the hero of your story
5. Simplify an issue or problem
6. Prompt an internal question or reflection

1. **Focus on "Why" instead of "What"**

   Why should your audience care about you? Why should they listen to your story? Wrestling this question to the ground requires you to go to a deeper and more emotional level of engagement by articulating not just what you do, but more importantly, **why** you do what you do. Most people focus on "what" they do but your audience wants to know "why" you are different from other people and "why" it matters to them. The "why" must speak to your core purpose. Why do you do what you do?

2. **Start with the Mind of Your Target Audience**

   Your brand story must be simple, clear and aligned with your audience's needs and wants. It must resonate with your audience in such a way that he or she wants to be a part of your brand story.

3. **Simplify an Issue or Problem**

   Does your "why" solve a problem? Does it articulate why your personal brand matters or the value that you bring to your audience? Most people have neither the time or inclination to figure this out on their own—this question needs to be answered through your "why."

4. **Stir Emotion in Your Audience**

   Give people a reason to care, a reason to pick you and a reason to stay.

People don't buy from making logical, rational buying decisions. They make emotional decisions and then justify those decisions by rationalizing them with facts. There is a huge difference between whether your audience views your story as just another transactional relationship or a story that emotionally connects with them.

5. Strike a Chord that Prompts an Internal Question or Reflection

What do you want people to think when they interact with your personal brand? People will be more engaged if they can relate to your story rather than listening to fact-laden statements about your credentials and accomplishments.

6. Make Your Audience the Hero of Your Story

Compelling stories resonate when the audience can put themselves at the center of the story. We must make the audience the hero while the brand assumes the role of a mentor. When your goal becomes participation rather than control, the hero is more likely to let you into their world.

What's Your Story?

Have you ever noticed when you ask someone to tell their personal story, they immediately launch into where they work or what they do?

The most successful business leaders have answers to that question which transcend the companies they work for and the products they sell. Their answer typically reveals a far deeper purpose in their lives. And oftentimes, a story that you want to be a part of.

Take a minute to think about the stories of two remarkable entrepreneurs: Henry Ford and Elon Musk. Entrepreneurs from different times, but entrepreneurs who share a similar vision.

Ford aspired to transform the market for automobiles, which at the time were expensive toys for the wealthiest few, into a mass marketed vehicle for the many.

Musk shared the same desire for his Tesla electric car in a 2013 TED Talk. "Our goal when we created Tesla a decade ago was the same as it is today: to accelerate the advent of sustainable transport by bringing compelling mass market electric cars to market as soon as possible."

Both of these well-known entrepreneurs have stories which are far bigger than the cars they manufactured and the brands they created. They have remarkable personal brand stories.

Ford was an industrialist and the father of the modern assembly line mode of production famous for saying that the customer could have "any color car, so long as it is black."

Musk is best known as an explorer, inventor and engineer. A multimillionaire before his 30th birthday, Musk is perhaps best known as the engineering brains behind the development of PayPal. Like Ford and Musk, those entrepreneurs who build a personal brand story worthy of remark—a story with purpose and passion—increase their chances of long-term success in life.

Of course, all of us have a personal brand story, whether you've consciously created one or not. It's absolutely essential to recognize this fact and be intentional about crafting your own story. A personal brand story is more than what you do for a living. It speaks to who you are and what you represent- it speaks to the core of *why you do what you do.*

To help you get started, here are three specific exercises you can take to write your own personal brand story:

Exercise 1: Discover Simplicity in Your Purpose (Your "Why")

Why do you do what you do? What is your purpose and what do you stand for?

Henry Ford believed civilization would only thrive and grow if people had reliable and affordable transportation. Elon Musk has taken a stand for a future with the masses utilizing transportation from clean, sustainable sources of energy.

Finding your "why" is not a straightforward task. You must evaluate your own values and beliefs to reveal your personal motivations—that which drives your behaviors. If your "why" centers on making a lot of money or just making enough to cover your bills, you have to dig deeper.

> *"An entrepreneur's drive is not about making money, but about making a difference in people's lives."*
>
> — Sir Richard Branson

You won't be able to build a business that can last if it doesn't mean more than money to you. Find your passion—the "why" that motivates you to jump out of bed every morning to take on the world.

Exercise 2: Bring Clarity to Action (Your "What")

Exercise 2 – Breakout in Pairs

The **Right** Story
What

Story

SIMPLICITY — What do you actually do?

CLARITY — What problems do you solve?

What do you do to demonstrate your 'why' to people?

ALIGNMENT — Does your 'what' change depending on the audience?

After you've discovered your "why," the next step is describing *what you do*. This doesn't necessarily mean you describe your industry or the type of business in which you currently work. If you only think about what you do in the context of your current situation, you will likely miss opportunities for breakthrough invention and innovation. You need a transformational "what"—the things that you do to enact the changes required to fulfill your "why."

If Henry Ford had limited the scope of his "what" to the manufacturing processes and technologies of his day, the Model T would never have been possible. He once famously said, "If I had asked people what they wanted, they would have said faster horses." Likewise, if Elon Musk had limited his scope to electric vehicle production standards and accepted the current state of battery technology, the Tesla would have never come to be.

> *"Transformation isn't about improving.*
> *It's about re-thinking"*
>
> – Malcolm Gladwell

The most remarkable personal stories are generally about a transformational journey. What traditions and norms must be challenged? What are the treacherous obstacles to overcome and the pitfalls to avoid? What overwhelming odds must be beat? Who are the "villains" that must be conquered? Who are the "dragons" that must be slayed along the way? By bringing this level of clarity to action you can create a more compelling and emotive story for yourself and the journey you want your audience to accompany you on.

Step 3: Make Your Audience the Hero (Your "How")

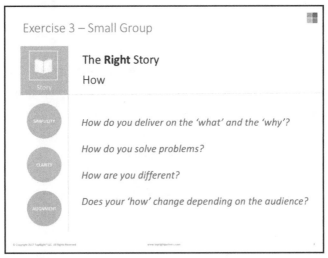

Keep in mind that <u>you are not the hero</u> of your own story. After all, you don't want to come across as a braggart!

This is not to suggest that successful entrepreneurs like Elon Musk, Richard Branson and Mark Cuban don't project a certain level of arrogance in how they intend to achieve their purpose. Quite the contrary, they most certainly do!

However, with their personal stories, successful entrepreneurs describe not only how they plan to achieve their "what", but they also invite their audience to become part of the story. If you doubt this, just ask a new Tesla owner about their personal role in reducing carbon emissions on the planet.

Compelling personal stories resonate when your audience can put themselves at the center of the stage. Your audience is the hero and you are simply the guide on the journey. Your story is not really about you. It is about the difference you make in other people's lives and how you guide them to a destination they could not otherwise reach on their own.

You must clearly state the outcomes and how you generate impact. Most people have neither the time nor the inclination to try to figure this out on their own. And if they are forced to figure this out for themselves, you have likely already lost them.

Remember that your personal brand story, is not about "closing the deal." It's about providing a few simple and clear sentences to open a doorway for your audience to walk through and engage with you. It should make them pause and consider what they have just seen or heard. In the few seconds that you have, they will not fully grasp the depth of your story. But if you have given them a reason to care, a reason to listen, and a reason to engage, they just might consider making your story a part of their own.

Always remember to ask yourself: does your personal brand story pass the test of simplicity, clarity, and alignment? Is your story so compelling that it can transform your listener into a storyteller on your behalf?

In his commencement speech to the Stanford class of 2005, Steve Jobs gave some simple but compelling advice to the graduates:

"You've got to find what you love. Your work is going to fill a large part of your life, and the only way to be truly satisfied is to do what you believe is great work. And the only way to do great work is to love what you do. If you haven't found it yet, keep looking. Don't settle."

— Steve Jobs

STRATEGY

Chapter 8

Formulating a Clear and Compelling Marketing Strategy

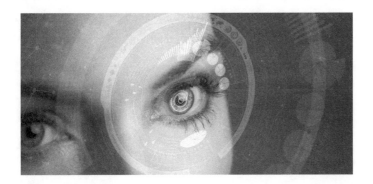

I f a tree falls in the forest and no one is around to hear it, does it make a sound? Not to open up a philosophical debate, but it is an interesting thought experiment for marketers to consider: If you tell a great brand story and no one is around to hear it, does it make a difference?

What if you tell a great brand story, but it's to the wrong people, or at the wrong time or in the wrong place? Do you make a difference?

A great brand story boils down the essence of why your brand should matter to people. It gives them a reason to care, a reason to buy, and a reason to stay.

Ideally, it compels them to respond on an emotional level.

But, what if that story never gets in front of the right people? What if it gets to the right people, but at the wrong time? Or through the wrong channel? What happens?

If you start a campaign to tell your brand story without a clearly defined strategy that targets the right audience and aligns with measurable business objectives, you're not going to make a significant impact.

Good marketers tell brand stories, great marketers tell them with purpose.

Consider the story of TLC Vision, a $300 million eye care services company. TLC held a leading position in the LASIK eye surgery industry thanks in large part to their simple brand story built around the promise of delivering life changing moments for patients. However, they lacked the right strategy to reach their target audience and give them a compelling reason to care, a reason to listen and a reason to come in for a consultation. They needed to get their story into the market in the most effective way to drive growth in consultations and LASIK eye surgery procedures.

What's a TLC Moment? It's a moment after having LASIK at TLC when it truly hits you—your life has changed forever thanks to clearer, crisper vision. It's the beginning of a more fulfilling life. If you've ever considered LASIK, or even just thought about it, now is the time to take the next step.

TLC's traditional go-to-market strategy was based primarily on receiving referrals from optometrists and ophthalmologists. A key competitor, LASIK Plus, disrupted the market by introducing a direct-to-consumer (DTC) advertising model. By circumventing the referring physician, LASIK Plus was able to build an authentic connection directly with the target audience and gather important insights about their needs and wants.

In order to keep up, TLC knew they had to complement their referral-based model with a new DTC model. However, TLC did not understand the different market segments, buyer personas or the steps patients took in making a decision to have LASIK surgery. Although they were an early adopter of blade-free LASIK technology, TLC did not believe it had fully leveraged the benefits of the new technology and were concerned that positioning was not clear with their target audience. Since they had been relying largely on referrals, they had limited data about consumers and their decision-making journey.

Market share was stable but recently TLC had ceded leadership to their key competitor. To tackle these challenges, TLC started by sharpening their brand story and focusing on their points of differentiation and preference at each point in the patient's decision-making process.

The TLC marketing team started with consumer research. They clearly defined different target segments, personas, and the LASIK decision journey of different segments of consumers. They refined their 6-second brand story and mapped differentiating benefits to each touch point in the decision-making journey to trigger desired consumer behaviors.

They were able to activate their segmentation strategy by developing a set of "golden questions" to identify which segment the consumer is a member of and reveal where they are in their own decision-making journey. The creative strategy focused on alleviating fears and concerns of the target audience with regard to safety and the quality of outcomes.

One of the high impact campaigns featured an endorsement from golf super-star Tiger Woods. Years earlier, Tiger's LASIK eye surgery had been performed by a TLC surgeon. It was a total coincidence. At the time, Tiger had a consultation and chose TLC just like any other patient and was provided no incentive to do so. If one of the most successful professional golfers of all time trusted his eyes to TLC, why not you? The authenticity and relevancy of the endorsement was particularly compelling for the more fearful target segments.

The results of the new strategy were dramatic. TLC Vision experienced an 18% increase in leads, consultations and procedures. They also saw a 50% increase in consumer awareness of the TLC brand. Most notably, their online consultation bookings grew from 5% to 15%. TLC had a great story—but a shift in their go-to-market strategy really brought their growth into focus.

Story without Strategy is Art; Story with Strategy is Marketing

If you feel like you have the right story, the next step is to clearly connect that story to your existing and prospective customers through formats that they consume, in channels that they use, across every touchpoint and at just the right stage in their buying journey.

As we saw in the story of TLC, you must develop an understanding of the customer and their decision-making journey. This enables you to activate your brand story through an integrated marketing strategy based on what really drives your customers to care, to engage, and to buy. It builds your story in a simple, clear and compelling way. Marrying the right story with the right strategy generates a profitable and productive customer experience. Profitable, because you are targeting customers who truly fit with your business, see the value of your products and services and are willing to pay a fair price to have that experience. Productive, because you meet your customers on their terms and enable them to make your brand story a part of their life story. Afterall, the two things that contribute most to winning in the marketplace are your brand story, and how your customers experience that story.

Winning Strategies Result in Profitable, Productive Customer Experiences

Creating a profitable and productive customer experience means that marketing must develop the specific content, offers and messages that are delivered at each "touchpoint" in the customer journey. Touchpoints include each and every customer interaction, from a first visit to your website to meeting with a salesperson to contacting customer service to renewing their contract to advocating for your brand.

A truly transformational marketing strategy is guided by your customers' interests and needs, and architected to respond to those interests with a more personalized experience. Again, your customer is at the center of the story and the center of your strategy. The goal? Create a remarkable customer experience that reflects the compelling nature of your brand story and cannot be easily copied by your competitors.

> *"By definition, remarkable things get remarked upon"*
> — Seth Godin

Transformational Marketing is Marketing That Sells

In many companies today, marketing is still primarily focused on the front end of the experience—generating leads. It's a bit like a relationship commitment problem—some marketers today are so focused on "dating," they don't know what to do after they've "closed the deal." And marketers without a remarkable customer experience will soon see their "dates" jumping ship as soon as something new and interesting—or maybe just a tad cheaper—comes along.

It's also worth noting that having a customer experience that just "feels good" or "entertains people" isn't worth much. If it's not generating money for your company, just focusing on the "fun" side of branding at the expense of hard science is like tossing fistfuls of cash out the window, music blasting, while driving down the highway. Fun, yeah. Profitable, no.

At its core, marketing is demand generation. Ads drive awareness…to drive sales. PR drives thought leadership…to drive sales. Social media drives communication…to drive sales.

Regardless of the tactic, the ultimate goal is to drive sales—selling more products and services to new customers or generating repeat business with existing customers. That's why Chief Marketing Officers (CMOs) are tasked with figuring out how to create not just good customer experiences, but also profitable and productive customer experiences.

Transformational marketing strategy requires a new mindset and a different blend of skills. Transformative marketers weave together the strategic focus and business analysis of a management consultant with the creativity and marketing expertise of a world-class agency. And, as we have noted, instead of focusing on the greatness of a company's products and services, the company positions the customer at the center of the universe.

This requires a deep and specific understanding of the customer, i.e., what the customer wants and needs at every stage of their decision-making journey. Transformative marketers invest in understanding the entire customer experience much better than their peers. They also have much better processes for capturing insights about customers and applying these insights to their marketing programs.

Customer Insights Power the Customer BuyWay

Customer experiences that are truly remarkable—and profitable—require a new approach to understanding the customer's journey. A transformative marketer knows how different segments of customers transit that journey, what their preferences are along the way and how to adjust tactics in real-time based on insights from actual customer behavior. This is the Customer BuyWay.

The Customer BuyWay leverages both qualitative and quantitative research to develop a comprehensive understanding of the infinitely more complex, non-linear, multi-channel, multi-device purchase process that is today's customer lifecycle. Unlike the popularized "Buyer's Journey," the Customer BuyWay doesn't end at the purchase stage, but rather encompasses the entire customer lifecycle, across every touchpoint.

Buyer's Journey vs. Customer BuyWay

Designed for simple, uncomplicated purchases	Comprehends more complex, longer purchase processes
Generally does not define each step of the purchase process	Dissects purchase process to define customer needs at each point
Identifies the overall benefit drivers for purchase intent	Identifies drivers of purchase intent at each decision point
Generally difficult to translate into a creative strategy beyond broad reach	Designed for activation — at broad reach and 1-to-1 level

The first step is to identify and define your target customers. This involves a segmentation of your target audience and the creation of ideal customer "profiles." These profiles, also known as buyer "personas," are based not only on customer and internal stakeholder interviews, but also quantitative survey data and customer behavioral analytics.

Key questions to ask during customer interviews might include:

- What are your core challenges and desired outcomes?

- Who, by role, has this need, challenge, desired outcome?

- Where do you go, both online as well as offline, for news, information and insights?

- When do you engage, either via marketing or sales call?

- How do you make decisions about purchasing products/services?

- Why would you choose our brand versus our competitor's brand?

Remember, this is only the first step.

Why not rely solely on this information alone? Interview and survey data can be imperfect. Employees and customers' mood and attention can play a factor or they may tell you what they think you want to hear.

The one thing that your customers or prospective customers can't hide? Their behavior. So, collecting and analyzing customer data across the organization— from tracking online engagement to what they purchase to how often they seek support— will arm you with the insights needed to begin translating your story to your customers through messages they seek, in formats that they consume, in channels that they use, across every touch point and at just the right stage in their BuyWay.

Segmenting by behavior opens up a constellation of possibilities for marketers. Instead of relying on static segments based on industry or role, it allows you to create dynamic segments based on how your customers actually behave. Not what we think they do. But what they actually do, mapped to their personas.

Navigating the Customer BuyWay

The path to purchase, repeat purchase and advocacy is no longer a direct route down the traditional sales funnel. It is now more like a spiral. Customers see, and engage with, many different types of content and messages at every stage and each interaction impacts the total result, for example:

- Social "likes" and reviews are factored into search rank

- Brand advertising increases click-through rates on search

- Bylined articles in targeted publications drive thought leadership and brand awareness

- Reviews increase confidence and influences organic search

- Blogging attracts more website visitors

BUYER'S JOURNEY FUNNEL

CUSTOMER BUYWAY SPIRAL

During the Awareness stage, customers are beginning to form opinions about their needs and considering what we refer to here as "Cost of Entry benefits." How can my problem be solved? What kind of outcomes do I need or expect? Should I even include your brand in my consideration set?

In the Consideration stage, customers have a better understanding of their specific needs and they are seeking to understand the "Differentiating benefits" of your brand—What makes you different from your competitors? What makes you different from the status quo?

And in the Decision stage, customers are judging their alternatives and the "Preference benefits" that help your brand come to the top of their short list— What's the difference in cost? How long will it take to get results? What are your customers saying about you?

In the Post-Sale "Advocate and Repeat" stage, customers seek not just satisfaction, but innovation, communication and support. What are the latest service and product updates? Are my questions being answered? What do I need to know to stay ahead of industry trends and best practices?

Each stage in your Customer BuyWay requires getting the right person, the right message, at the right time. Nothing is more frustrating to customers than spending countless hours doing research only to find themselves back at square one with your company's representative in an introductory conversation. According to CEB, buyers are 57 percent of the way through their purchase process before they even reach out to talk to someone at a company. These frustrations are caused by a lack of Strategy and insight into the behavior of prospective customers.

In order to be truly transformational and interrupt marketing as usual, you must establish a clear strategy to tell a simple, clear and aligned story to the right person, at the right time, through the proper channel.

Chapter 9

Personifying Your Strategy

C had Thevenot, Executive Director of The Institute for Humane Studies (IHS), believes in the power of freedom to enable people to unleash their unique potential and help create a more just, peaceful and thriving world. Now that's a powerful personal "why" statement!

Under Chad's leadership, IHS inspires students and professors to engage with the ideas of freedom. Furthermore, IHS supports people in advancing the principles and practices of freedom in their careers and connects them to a community of individuals committed to the power of freedom, open inquiry and idea exchange. The overall goal is to broaden on-campus conversations and encourage the exploration of ideas beyond the current perceived bias toward liberalism at Universities.

The target audience for IHS programs and offerings includes undergraduates who have demonstrated an interest in their studies to pursue a career in higher education. They also target graduate students who are on a career path in

INSTITUTE FOR **HUMANE STUDIES**
AT GEORGE MASON UNIVERSITY

Q *Why does IHS exist?*

We believe in the power of freedom to enable people to unleash their unique potential and help create a more just, peaceful, and thriving world.

Q *What does IHS do?*

Q *How does IHS do this?*

We inspire students and professors to engage with the ideas of freedom. We support them in advancing the principles and practice of freedom in their careers. We connect them to a community of individuals committed to the power of freedom and of ideas.

We inspire and educate college students throughout their student experience.	• Advanced Topics in Liberty (weekend conferences) • *Learn Liberty* Videos • *Learn Liberty* Online Seminars • On-Campus Programs (seminars, speakers, discussion groups, book clubs) • Summer Seminars • Harper Internship Program
We connect talent to opportunities.	• *Learn Liberty* Opportunities for Students (Online Opportunities Bank) • Online Academic Hub • Roger Pilon Fellowship
We support future professors.	• Career Development Seminars (grad and undergrad) • Current Research Workshops • Hayek Fund for Scholars • Humane Studies Fellowship • Mentoring • Online Academic Programs • PhD Fee Waiver • PhD Scholarship • Placement Support • Research and Conference Grants • Research Colloquia (grad and undergrad) • Summer Graduate Research Fellowship
We facilitate the impact of professors across and beyond campus.	• Find Scholars • Hayek Fund for Scholars • On-Campus Faculty Partnership • Policy Research Seminars
We partner with allies and supporters to advance freedom.	• Partnerships with Allied Organizations • Donor Events • Donor Outreach and Communications

Q *In 5 years, what will IHS have accomplished?*

The Post

July 23, 2020

IHS Impacts Academia, Policy

IHS and a Community of Freedom-Inspired Professors Have Changed the Conversation Among Students and on Campus, and Impacted the Policy Arena

theihs.org

The IHS Brand Story

academia, as well as "freedom-friendly" faculty members who are seeking support and a broader platform for sharing their ideas. Concurrently, IHS targets like-minded organizations and individuals for their financial support of these candidates and the organization's programs that support both the students and the academic institutions.

With a simple, clear and compelling brand story to tell, Chad's attention shifted to formulating a strategy for IHS to reach the right target at the right time, with the right message to trigger the right behaviors.

IHS had conducted traditional market segmentation studies in the past to gain a deeper understanding of students, faculty and donors. However, the data generated from those studies had not been particularly useful. A lot of interesting facts were generated but few actionable insights. General demographic data about the different segments was helpful for targeting, but the research yielded very little with regard to what actually drives people's behaviors in their academic and professional careers.

No, traditional marketing research just wasn't going to cut it. So, Chad decided to take a different approach.

He aimed to "personify" each segment of the IHS audience to truly reveal their preferences and the subtle distinctions in their behaviors. With fully developed personas, Chad knew that IHS would be able to tailor its messaging to be more relevant and authentic to the needs and wants of the individual. Moreover, Chad wanted to gain a deeper understand of their decision-making journey (i.e. BuyWay). And as appropriate, IHS could create experiences to engage them and make the IHS brand story a part of their own personal academic stories.

The output of this important work had to be actionable and answer several key questions like:

- What motivates the target to learn?
- Where do their interests lead them?
- What does IHS have to offer?
- How do they make decisions?
- Where are they in their journey?
- What do we need to say or offer to engage them?
- What should we be measuring to evaluate performance?

Alex

The Liberty Leader—very aligned with IHS brand story

What motivates Alex to learn?

- Getting to learn about personally interesting topics, networking, and having the opportunity to learn on campus

Where do his interests lead him?

- On his mobile phone

- Leading a campus group

What does IHS have to offer to Alex?

- Share our more intensive Learn Liberty products

What do we need to say to Alex to engage him?

- We represent a safe place to express, openly debate, and cultivate ideas

Through this strategic work, IHS was able to identify a highly actionable segment of their target audience on college campuses today who they called the "Liberty Leader." Here is a brief overview of the persona that they developed for *Alex*:

Alex is energetic and enthusiastic, and carries this passion into the learning environment. He has a strong sense of personal responsibility and accountability. He likes being on campus and enjoys interacting with his fellow students and professors.

He is equally as comfortable participating in classroom lectures and workshops, as watching an educational video online in his dorm room. He is passionate about his beliefs, which are often influenced by his immigrant family background, and is typically among the first to offer an opinion or lead a classroom discussion.

He is active on social media, and relies heavily on mobile technology to keep pace with his busy day. If something needs to get done, Alex is your go-to-guy.

Armed with this deeper level of insight, Chad's marketing team at IHS was able to create far more relevant and engaging messaging for Alex on college campuses across the country. By understanding Alex's journey and communication preferences with greater precision, IHS could create experiences for Alex that are more relevant to him. Rather than interrupting Alex with irrelevant or unnecessary messages, IHS could give Alex precisely what he needed in order to move him to the next phase of his journey.

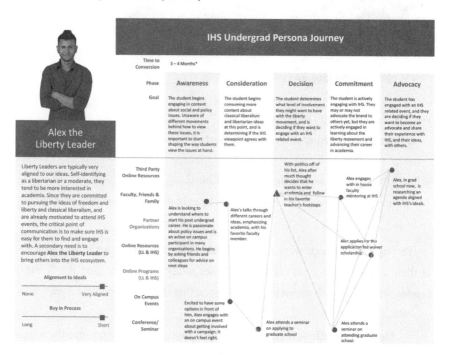

By building out personas, Chad's marketing team also discovered that there are people on college campuses today that are just not a good fit for the IHS brand story. Identifying these audience members meant that the organization did not have to waste precious time and resources trying to "persuade the unpersuadable."

Chad and his team have now applied the new personification strategy to all of their target audiences—undergraduates, graduates, faculty and donors.

As a result, IHS campaigns are highly efficient, differentiated and tailored for each persona within each target segment. Personas embody not only what people say they want, but also reveal what truly motivates their behavior to take action. IHS is creating remarkable experiences for their customer by giving them a highly personalized reason to care, a reason to engage, a reason to openly share the ideas of freedom and a reason to advocate for the organization.

How Do You Personify Your Marketing Strategy?

As we saw with the IHS case, traditional market segmentation didn't go far enough to give Chad and his team actionable insight to drive student, faculty and donor engagement.

The traditional statistical approach to developing targeted segments through marketing research requires only a basic understanding of statistics and relies heavily on the responses that consumers or customer provide to survey questions.

What's wrong with that?

At its heart, there's nothing wrong with developing targeted segments based on how your consumers or customers respond to surveys. For many companies, even this step can represent a quantum leap from simply guessing at demographics or relying on anecdotes.

However, for transformative marketers who have a more sophisticated grasp of the two powerful levers of segmentation and differentiation, transformational approaches to segmentation offer a lot more.

After you've performed a more traditional segmentation, you realize that you're playing with only a small set of information about your target audience and there's great risk that you're going to go far astray from the actionable insights that you are seeking.

Your customers and consumers might be in a bad mood when they take the survey. Or, worse, they're just pre-occupied, or maybe gaming the system, or just trying to tell you what you want to here. Maybe you're only getting the people that are in the mood to complete surveys or have a lot of spare time.

The one thing that your customers or prospects can't hide? Their behavior.

Segmenting by behavior opens up a constellation of possibilities for marketers. Instead of putting your consumers or customers into immutable segments based on who they are or how they think, it's infinitely better to create changeable segments based on how your consumer or customers behave.

Enough with a handful of static segments, why aren't you and your company creating hundreds of segments and corresponding personas, permitting your customers to move from segment to segment based on their specific behaviors and where they happen to be in their decision-making journey? What you will discover is that your customer's actual behaviors will put them into specific segments that will demand a very specific marketing response. **You'll also see your marketing effectiveness increase dramatically as you stop interrupting people and instead, meet them on their terms with timely and relevant messaging.**

Segmentation by behavior and developing unique personas—getting beyond simplistic, survey-driven segments—will give you the understanding of your customers to deliver the right message, to the right target, at the right time. In other words, it's critical to maximizing your return on marketing investments. Why invest in communicating your brand story to people that are never going to buy? Likewise, why alienate the right buyers by assuming that all people in a certain segment want to engage with you in the same way?

Behavior driven segments can give you the advantage that you're looking for—and analytical tools are readily available for you to bring a more modern and sophisticated approach to marketing to your targeted customers. If you're a retailer, how much is it worth to identify customer behaviors that lead to attrition—and provide a window for you to invest in keeping them in the fold? If you're a financial services company, how much is it worth to know what behaviors indicate that consumers are in the market for specific products and services (and give you the go ahead to cross-sell products that are highly likely to be appealing)?

Of course, you can stick with turning survey responses into segments and give them funny names like Discount Diva or Upscale Hipsters. Alternatively, you can use real customer behavior data to create behavior-based segments and personas; dispense with the funny names, and just get down to business driving sales and profits higher.

Building behavioral segments and personas can be tricky – it's important to have the right balance between quantitative and qualitative data to get an accurate and actionable profile. With an accurate buyer persona, marketers are able to target their message to subsets of customers with common needs and interests. Sophisticated analytical techniques that can be used to identify patterns and convert unstructured data into actionable insights, allowing the creation of buyer personas for highly targeted and effective individualized marketing campaigns.

Here is a simple example to demonstrate how this works and to highlight the power of text analytics to build personas and reveal actionable insights for marketers:

Translating Patterns into Personas

With the 2016 U.S. Presidential race in the rearview mirror (but still the subject of hot debate on the evening news!), we thought it would be interesting to explore what, if any, patterns in the way people describe themselves could be used to identify their "political personas." For instance, are there characteristics that might predict whether you are a Democrat or a Republican?

For this example, OdinText, a powerful text analytics application, was used to identify several striking and statistically significant **differences** between the way Republicans and Democrats describe themselves.

Let me emphasize that this exercise had nothing to do with demographics: gender, age, ethnicity, income, etc. We're all aware of the statistical demographic differences between Republicans and Democrats. Specific demographic information people shared in describing themselves was only pertinent to the extent that it constituted a broader response pattern that could predict political affiliation.

When it comes to self-image, there are significant differences.

As it turns out, Republicans were significantly more likely than Democrats to say they have blonde hair. However, this does not necessarily mean that someone with blonde hair is significantly more likely to be a Republican; rather, it simply means that if you have blonde hair, you are significantly more likely to feel it noteworthy to mention when describing yourself, if you are a Republican than if you are a Democrat.

Republicans are far more likely to include their marital status, religion, ethnicity and education level in describing themselves, and to mention that they are charitable/generous.

Democrats, on the other hand, are significantly more likely to describe themselves in terms of friendships, work ethic and the quality of their smile.

Deeper analysis turned up several predictors for party affiliation as portrayed below:

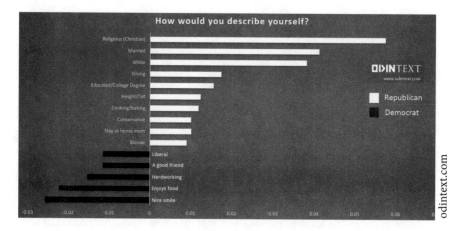

Interestingly, this research identified quite a few more predictors for Republicans than Democrats, suggesting that the former may be more homogeneous in terms of which aspects of their identities matter most. This translates to a somewhat higher level of confidence in predicting affinity with the Republican Party.

For instance, if you describe yourself as both "Christian" and "married," without knowing anything else about you, it can be assumed with 90 percent accuracy that you vote Republican.

Again, this does not mean that Christians who are married are more than 90 percent likely to be Republicans, but it does mean that people who mention these two things when asked to tell a stranger about themselves are extremely likely to be Republicans.

So what?

Could a political campaign put this capability to work segmenting likely voters and targeting messages? Absolutely! But the application obviously extends well beyond politics.

While this simple example was exploratory and the results should not be taken as definitive, it demonstrates that text analytics tools make it entirely possible to read between the lines and determine far more about customers than marketers previously thought was possible.

People are increasingly expecting brands to deliver real-time, relevant messages. As a result, the discipline of marketing is rapidly transforming to personalized and individualized marketing, requiring marketers to understand the customer as an individual persona, quickly adapt to each customer's changing needs, and execute marketing initiatives at a personal level.

According to Teradata, 80 percent of marketers agree that individualized marketing is a top priority. However, only 43 percent of marketers say that they are delivering individualized experiences for their customers. These sophisticated predictive model techniques help close the gap between the strategy and execution of an effective individualized marketing campaign.

"Personifying your marketing strategy is not an option, it's a customer expectation"

With an exponentially-increasing flood of customer satisfaction data, customer experience touchpoints, CRM transactions, and consumer-generated social media text, there is no shortage of data available. The data and the tools are there. And transformative marketers are using them to predictively model all manner of customer behaviors to help them personify their marketing strategies. The result? They're moving to the TopRight quadrant of performance in the markets where the choose to compete.

Chapter 10
Entering New and Emerging Markets

When the popular casual shoe brand Crocs entered the India market in 2007, it assumed the conditions for rapid and profitable growth were in place. Crocs struck an exclusive joint venture deal with a local partner, which subsequently evolved into a franchising arrangement as leadership wanted to capitalize on an opportunity to expand quickly. However, despite preliminary enthusiasm, the arrangement was far from successful. After eight years, the brand only had 30 stores in India. Because sales didn't meet expectations, Crocs was forced to cancel the exclusive franchising agreement and recently announced the closure of 12 stores.

"We planned out a strategy of having a few, but strong, franchisees and shedding some of the partners that don't, can't, or won't want to grow with us whatever reason."

— Nissan Joseph, GM of Crocs India

Crocs India still has a presence in 100 cities across the country through its ecommerce channel, its exclusive stores, department stores, footwear chains, and mom & pop retailers. However, the company wasted several years and significant marketing investments. Crocs India must focus now on building more reliable distribution channels, making more effective marketing investments, and re-engaging Indian customers through local subsidiaries. So, where did they go wrong?

"Here lies one who meant well, tried a little, failed much: surely that may be his epitaph, of which he need not be ashamed."

– Robert Lewis Stevenson, *Across the Plains*

The Traditional Approach to Global Emerging Market Entry

For decades, many multinational brands have tried to venture into emerging markets. To limit risk, companies often partner with a local distributor, a critical first step to market entry success. In most cases, distributors achieve quick wins and rapid sales growth by placing the products in their existing network. The novelty of having new offerings in the channel leads to initial success. However, rapid revenue growth often turns into disappointment soon thereafter. Why does this happen?

To minimize their risk, brands only invest a tiny percentage into local marketing. They assume the distributor will pay marketing and brand building from its share of the profits. This challenge presents itself as the company attempts to sustain the growth and the "blame-game" starts between company managers and the distributor.

Faced with declining sales, the company terminates the distribution agreement and blames the failure on the distributor and its lack of product knowledge, hands-on involvement, or financial ineptitude. This is often a hasty, misinformed decision that leads to compounding mistakes.

Because the company blames the distributor for mediocre performance, it then believes it has the market knowledge and capabilities to launch its own subsidiary in the country. **This is an expensive and disruptive process that often leads to market exit as the company overplays its hand, fails to recognize its blind spots, and overestimates its understanding of the market.**

This is a common phenomenon for multinationals expanding into new emerging markets like India.

In our experience at TopRight, we have witnessed too many multinational brands rush to sell and scale, and then fail. Successful global emerging market entry requires a step-by-step, disciplined emerging market strategy that establishes a foundation for sustained growth. The graphic below illustrates the traditional approach that multinational brands take for entering an emerging market.

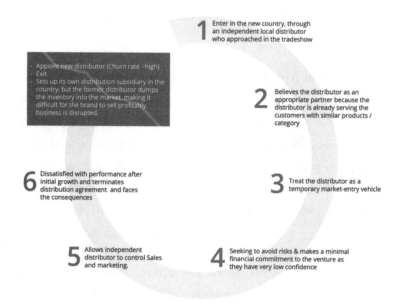

Following this traditional approach, the negative outcomes are predictable:

- Local market doesn't understand the brand story and the core values of the brand

- Overly complicated communication strategy confuses the market

- Marketing investment is focused on closing deals rather than conditioning the market

- e-Commerce channels are misused—failing to educate and serve customers

- After sales customer service is insufficient—leading to customer dissatisfaction

- Negative word of mouth spreads quickly in emerging markets

- Distributors cut prices to liquidate and dump excess inventory in the market

Not surprisingly, initial sales success is rarely sustained and the potential to tarnish the brand image is high.

The Transformational Approach to Emerging Market Entry

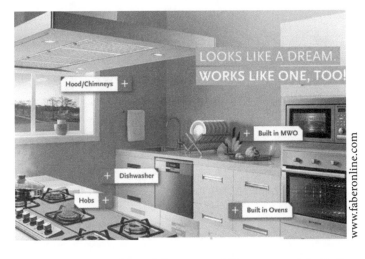

Let's examine a multinational brand that successfully penetrated the India market and fared much better than Crocs.

In 1997, Faber saw an opportunity in the developing Indian market. The company made an entry through a local distributor with one product: kitchen hoods. It increased brand strength by expanding its offerings to other products like built-in hobs and premium cooking ranges in early 2000. Through a joint-venture, Faber later established a decorative chimney manufacturing plant.

Today, Faber is India's No.1 Hoods and Hobs brand. Over 250 employees produce more than 300 products in the local plant with current production capacity of 150,000 hoods, 100,000 hobs, and 50,000 other kitchen appliances per annum. Recognizing the importance of an extensive network towards building a long-term success story, Faber has over 2,000 retail counters for sales and service across the country. It has achieved economies of scale and has been able to sustain a competitive edge against most of the cooking equipment brands worldwide.

Unlike Crocs, the Faber leadership team identified the right local partner who was the right fit for the company's global emerging market strategy. The company collaborated with the local partner, encouraged the distributor to lead all initiatives, and made investments in a disciplined, phased manner. Faber retained control of the marketing strategy from the beginning and actively anticipated market changes, resulting in a better brand image, less crisis, and consistent growth.

Here is a graphic representation of the transformational approach that Faber took as they entered the Indian market.

Establishes own subsidiary in the new country, and builds relationship among distributors, as a result leveraging synergies and economies across the company. Position and market brands where local consumers can relate and ultimately own

6 Leverage its global competitive advantages in the local market. Because the local partner regularly furnishes detailed market and financial performance data

1 Chooses the market based on objective assessments and initial market assessment.

5 Involves in developing regional marketing strategy and works with the local distributor on market development

2 Evaluate different market entry routes and choose the one which fits for their industry. Looks for one with a "good company fit"- Culture and Strategy compatible.

4 Makes an upfront commitment and significant investment.

Phase 2 - Conduct in-depth market research and consumer insights

3 Collaboratively works with local leadership team and encourages them to initiate marketing and development projects.

Treat the local partner as a long-term partner

Brand 2 works collaboratively with the local partner and encourage them to lead all initiatives. However, it retains control of the marketing strategy from the beginning and anticipate changes. This will result in high brand image, less crisis and consistent growth.

Following the transformational approach, many of the emerging market risks can be mitigated and the negative outcomes can be avoided:

- Local market understands the brand story and how it makes them "a hero"

- Simple and clear communication strategy is easy for the market to embrace

- Some of the marketing investment is focused on conditioning the market

- e-Commerce channels are enablers to educate and serve customers

- After sales customer service is robust and identifies advocates—leading to customer delight

- Positive word of mouth spreads quickly in emerging markets

- Distributors understand that price-cutting to liquidate and dump excess inventory in the market must be avoided

In contrasting these two brand examples, there is an important lesson to be learned. Emerging market entry mistakes are not just related to selecting the wrong distribution partner. You could select exactly the right partner and still fail. Success relies on your marketing mindset and the discipline that you exercise as you enter a new market. **To increase the likelihood of success, multinational brands should embrace a transformational marketing approach from the beginning.** The winning strategy lies in continuous changes during and after market entry by anticipating and adapting to challenges.

It's easy to make mistakes. But as we learned with Faber in India, a practical, strategic and systematic emerging market entry playbook is required to help brands reduce their risks, maximize their ROI, compete efficiently, and win in emerging marketplaces. With a global vision, hands-on experience, and local network, you can acquire valuable market information, undertake comprehensive market analyses, formulate appropriate entry strategy, find best routes-to-market, establish distribution channels, and rapidly grow your business in new and emerging markets.

Chapter 11

Extending Your Brand

www.alamy.com

I magine walking into a grocery store, choosing your items, and walking out. No lines. No checkout. No price checks. No money changing hands.

If that seems like grocery-shopping heaven, then you're going to love the latest from Amazon: "Just Walk Out Shopping." Completely rethinking the shopping experience, Amazon Go employs innovative technology to create a seamless, unique, and delightful customer experience. This strategic use of technology removes all of the friction in the Customer's BuyWay—enabling a customer to walk into the store, grab their groceries, and walk-out without the hassle of checkout lines.

Understanding buying habits of individual consumers to provide more personalized marketing has been a challenge for grocery stores and retailers for years.

Amazon Go solves this problem with an analytics-first approach to the in-store customer experience. Not only does this fuel individualized marketing, it also provides Amazon with the highly-coveted singular view of individual customer buying habits, both online and offline. Although this isn't Amazon's first attempt at brick and mortar, it's a logical fit and aligns with the current brand values of convenience and innovation. As we now know, Amazon Go was just a rehearsal for the main act: Amazon's acquisition of Whole Foods Markets.

Are you ready to have your granola and freshly-ground coffee gently placed at your doorstep by a drone? That dream may have become one step closer with this deal. Considering the volume and distribution of Whole Foods stores, this acquisition will also mean a much faster expansion of Amazon's Walkout Technology. Combined, these two strategic moves by Amazon may turn out to be one of the great brand extension examples of all time (or potentially the biggest flop if they fail to personify their strategy!).

A brand extension strategy (found at the #TopRight corner of the matrix below), leverages the parent brand to enter a new product category.

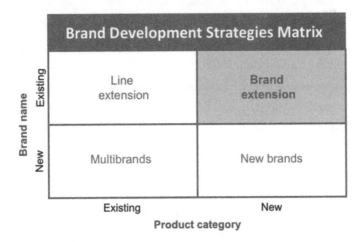

When compared to the launch of a new brand, this strategy adds incremental value and reduces risk and costs. Like the Amazon example, brand extension is more common for firms whose current brand equity is strong enough to influence the existing customer base and grant permission to extend into new product and service categories.

There are many conditions for success that must be in place to execute a successful brand extension strategy. The general consensus is that when brand equity is high, the chances of a successful brand extension increase. Based on this fact, there are higher chances of a positive launch for well-known brands. On the other hand, there are a number of examples in the market of how even the most well-known and well-established brands have failed. Almost 84% of brand extensions fail and, of the successes, only 54% survive after the third year, proving that the success relies on a number of factors. Brand extensions in the hospitality industry serve as good support for these statistics.

Consider the example of the global market leader in quick serve restaurants: McDonald's. Do you remember when McDonalds launched their now infamous "Golden Arch" hotel with the catchy tagline: "be with us"? The four-star hotel located in Zurich that closed just two and a half years later? Well, we can attribute one of the reasons of the failure to a low brand association between the parent brand and a four-star type of hotel. Although the venture loosely related to the company's food business and relied on many of its core hospitality competencies, such as franchising and real estate management, the McDonald's brand doesn't square with the image of a four-star hotel. That brand extension was just a "bridge too far" in the mind of the customer. Why would I trust a purveyor of burger and fries to handle my travel accommodations?

On the other hand, if you are a "luxury boutique" type of hotel guest, would you consider staying at hotels by Equinox (the luxury fitness gym operator), West Elm and Restoration Hardware (home good retailers)? You might be thinking: these are all non-hospitality brands so why should I consider them for my hotel selection? In fact, all three have entered the hospitality industry. These brands are venturing into the risky world of brand extensions, planning to launch boutique hotels in different locations in the U.S over the next several years.

In a widely competitive environment, companies are trying to expand their reach to new customers, reinforce their value, and efficiently grow their business. Among the various types of organic growth strategies, a brand development approach highlights existing and new opportunities.

Are these going to become successful brand extensions? Will customers give them permission to extend into these new offerings? It's hard to tell at this point.

What about luxury brands like Armani, Versace, Bulgari and Ferragamo? All of these companies possess very high brand equity and they are relevant in a luxury niche that could succeed in the hospitality industry. Yet their potential for success might also be questioned. One of the key reasons: all of them are strong luxury brands, but operating hotels is clearly not their core competency. Bulgari, on the other hand, had a different strategy, which set them apart from the pack and made their brand extension more successful. The difference? The company created a joint venture with a hospitality expert: Marriott hotels, which reduces their risk and increases their probability of success.

The reality is that there are many examples of successful brand extensions, and the benefits from the extensions are huge. Beyond offering new sources of revenue, a successful brand extension can create business diversification, achieve marketing efficiencies between categories, increase brand equity, enhance brand associations and accelerate the speed to market the new category.

But it turns out that there are several conditions for success that must be maintained for you to succeed. So, here are six tips to help guide you on your brand extension journey:

6 TIPS for SUCCESS FOR BRAND EXTENSION

1. Measure brand equity to understand the chances of a successful launch

2. Measure potential risks and identify the positive and negative effects

3. Leverage from your core competencies and establish partnerships when necessary

4. Invest in marketing research and assess the market potential of the new category

5. Make the brand extension a logical fit to the existing brand

6. Create a compelling go-to-market strategy to connect with your audience

1. **Measure Brand Equity**

   One of the biggest concerns when implementing brand extensions is the risk of causing brand dilution, that is, when the new product category fails and presents a negative impact on the brand as a whole. Thus, the first step is to have a Brand Equity measurement in place in order to track possible future impacts.

2. **Measure the potential risks**

   Run a scenario analysis to identify the positive or negative effects on the business and brand equity. The goal is to implement a brand extension whose risk of failure does not exceed any marketing efficiencies.

3. **Leverage your core competencies**

   The new product should leverage all the skills and know-how from the current business and marketing operations in order to gain a competitive advantage in the new category. By identifying the business key competencies, the brand will be able to gain efficiencies and create market differentiation.

4. **Invest in Marketing Research**

   In the eagerness to grow the business, brands forget about making sure the new category has market potential, that there are clear opportunities or unmet customer needs. When identifying key opportunities, make sure to understand prospect and current customers and estimate their acceptance for potential brand acceptance. Use marketing research also to test the possible new brand extensions.

5. **Make the brand extension a logical fit**

   The new product must be a logical fit to the brand, compatible, expected and follow the current brand story. The link between the new product and the parent brand should be easily tracked. The biggest brand extension pitfalls fall into this category.

6. Create a Brand Extension Strategy

After making sure the story follows a smooth path between both categories, make sure you develop a brand management plan and a compelling go-to-market strategy that will connect with your audience across multiple touchpoints on the Customer BuyWay.

There will always be uncertainty about how successful a brand extension can be. Will West Elm and Restoration Hardware leverage its furniture know-how and integrate it successfully in the hospitality industry? And, will Equinox have a successful connection between the hospitality industry and its health and wellness experience? Each of these brands plan to launch new hotel locations before 2020. Until then, we will continue analyzing whether their brand extension strategies will pay off or not.

Moving your business to TopRight performance with a successful brand extension strategy requires a deep understanding of your brand and your customers. Not only should you assess if the new business is a logical fit, but also you must refine your brand story and communicate to your customers to validate that you've earned their permission to make the transformation into a completely new market or category.

Chapter 12

Creating Remarkable Customer Experiences

www.flickr.com/photos/
spackletoe/90811910

What if creating remarkable customer experiences was as easy as pushing a button?

The "Easy Button" has become a marketing icon for Staples, the office supply retailer. It is a wonderfully simple manifestation of their Brand Story and it clearly and succinctly communicates the brand promise of being "easy to do business with"—a perfect example of a six-second story. But let's face it: we're talking about a red plastic button that says, "that was easy" when you press it. At last count, Staples has sold over 8 million of these things. Impressive indeed, but what real, measurable impact has that had on Staples' customer experience (CX)?

With an 800-lb gorilla like Amazon breathing down your neck every day, you need more than a red plastic toy to win in a highly competitive and commoditizing market.

When Faisal Masud joined Staples as Chief Digital Officer in 2015, his mandate was clear: follow B2B shoppers moving online and meet their demands by doubling down on digital… and make it easy!

Staples has had a digital presence since 1998 — long before many other retailers — but Masud's ambition was to take it to the next level and create a seamless omni-channel customer experience. He knew that just supporting multiple channels for customers would be insufficient. Staples would have to be sure that all channels would connect to one another.

"The goal for Staples has been to be a unified view of the customer, where we are completely agnostic to where customers shop, offline or in the stores, on their phone or on their desktop, or through any other means, and really making sure that we personalize that experience to them."
— Faisal Masud, Chief Digital Officer at Staples

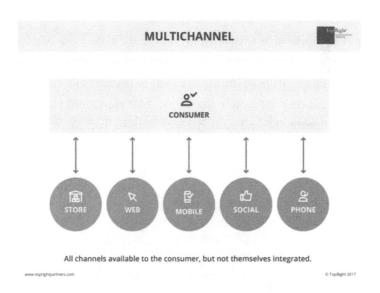

MULTICHANNEL

CONSUMER

STORE   WEB   MOBILE   SOCIAL   PHONE

All channels available to the consumer, but not themselves integrated.

www.toprightpartners.com   © TopRight 2017

One of the biggest challenges of omni-channel is resolving the deal-breaking frustration customers experience when they are forced to engage separately with the online and offline pieces of the same business, from deals and coupon offers to product purchases and returns.

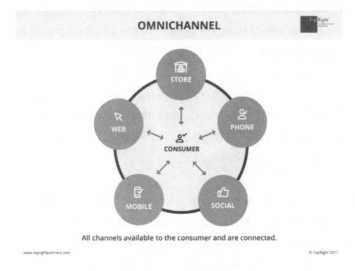

All channels available to the consumer and are connected.

www.toprightpartners.com   © TopRight 2017

Watson IBM and AI Powered Chatbots Reinforce Staples' Brand Story

The Staples team started by attempting to reduce some of the friction in their customer service department by building an online chat function using IBM Watson. The brand leveraged artificial intelligence tools to answer basic customer questions in real time on their mobile app. Staples later announced plans to extend the chat functionality beyond customer service to support more sophisticated customer ordering experiences on its website, through Facebook Messenger and via Slack.

www.staples.com

With the quick success of the chatbot enhancing the customer experience, Masud's team moved on to a much bigger challenge: transforming their iconic Easy Button into an intelligent, voice-driven interface that allows customers to reorder office supplies with minimum human interaction. In a single afternoon, Staples built a simple but effective and engaging conversational platform using Watson services to link the Easy Button with a customer's online shopping cart.

"A critical component of Watson's technology is engagement, facilitating better interactions between brands and consumers, deepening connections, and enhancing how people engage,"
— Steve Abrams, Vice President of Developer
Advocacy at IBM Watson

But Masud and his team have not stopped there. They continue to build out the technology to include natural language processing and analytics tools from Watson. Today, the Easy Button is truly living up to its iconic promise: making it far easier for any customer to place an order and get access to other Staples services, anytime, anywhere.

However, as Masud has pointed out in his public comments, **successfully delivering an omni-channel customer experience has more to do with breaking down barriers in the organization rather than beating the competition with technology.**

"The biggest challenge retail faces is not Amazon — it's actually the structure within, that setup where the store location and the online business are completely siloed and essentially combating each other. And it doesn't work for the customer. Because the customer is looking at the retailer with one lens: Can I shop with them any which way I want?"
— Faisul Masud, Chief Digital Officer at Staples

And that's where Staples is headed next. They are exploring how to "fingerprint" customers across channels—stitching together all the valuable customer data they must have to provide a cohesive, personalized experience regardless of channel touchpoint. For companies like Staples with lots of retail locations, this is a major barrier to overcome. Fingerprinting a store customer requires attaching an identity to every shopper who walks through the door. No one's nailed the algorithm for this yet, but Staples is working on it!

User Experience (UX) is a subset of the overall Customer Experience (CX)

With 97 percent of consumers indicating their purchasing decisions are influenced by an online experience, it's evident that user experience (UX) is now inextricably linked to the overall customer experience. Just as living the brand message extends beyond the marketing department, so too, has UX extended beyond the domain of the web design and development.

Customers don't care when they start browsing in one place and end up purchasing in another — but you need to.

Moreover, a good user experience is no longer a nice-to-have; it's an expectation, as illustrated by the 89 percent of consumers who said they would switch to a competitor if an online experience was poor. To transform your customers into brand advocates, a positive user experience must be part of every interaction a consumer has with your brand.

While having an aesthetically pleasing UX may initially drive ROI and conversion, the overall customer experience is what drives repeat business and brand attachment.

When preparing a user experience strategy, knowing your buyer personas and understanding the Customer BuyWay as it relates to each persona is essential. Only after you understand this can you design a customer experience strategy that makes the consumer the hero.

Gables Residential is a great example of a brand strategically using UX to make the customer the hero, enable sales, and create a seamless customer experience both online and offline. By approaching the problem through the eyes of the consumer, Gables was able to find a way to delight customers and convert sales.

The company developed an iPad sales application that gave leasing agents tools that covered the entire lead to lease process. The sales app is integrated with the customer-facing search tool which enables customers to search properties in real-time and then forward the search preferences and profile to the agent. By making the prospects' lives easier, the brand successfully positions itself as the guide to empower customers to arrive at their desired destination.

UX must be fully aligned with your Brand Story and Strategy

Your brand story must be incorporated into every aspect of the user experience, online and offline. Each touchpoint should align with your brand story in a way that speaks to your customers and invites them to engage.

Apple, one of the world's most valuable companies, is renowned for its stellar design and product UX. But, even for Apple, pretty design and good aesthetics alone aren't enough. Its brand story is aligned across the organization and incorporated into every aspect of the user experience.

From hardware to software, applications, and in-store experience, the simplicity and clarity of Apple's messaging is intertwined throughout the whole customer experience. In its stores, laptop screens are adjusted to a recommended angle that causes a glare, so prospective customers have to adjust the screen to see it. This multi-sensory experience increases buyer interaction with the products and helps evoke a sense of ownership pre-purchase. Apple's consistency in user experience increases brand attachment.

A transformational user experience is clearly aligned with a brand's story and strategy.

The marketers and leaders who are innovating and transforming the customer experience understand that UX goes far beyond digital design. It's a sales enablement tool, an opportunity to create customer experiences that engage and delight, and a vital subset of the overall customer journey. **In order to create an effective and revenue-generating UX strategy, you must distill your brand story down to six seconds.**

So, what can be learned from Apple, Gables and Staples omnichannel experiences?

First, we all must acknowledge that customer experience is at the heart of every business. No matter what your business does and how you do it, your customers are what keeps your business going. Finding new and innovative ways to engage with them and make their experience better is what every company must strive to do.

By adopting an omni-channel mindset and answering two key questions, you can begin to uncover new opportunities to create remarkable customer experiences:

1. **Do you have a unified view of the customer?**

   As we learned in the Staples case, an organization must have a unified view of the customer. That view must be completely agnostic to where customers shop—offline or in-store, on their mobile device or on their desktop—so you can personalize and optimize the customer experience. There is nothing more frustrating for a customer than having to share their same information with your team over-and-over to complete a single transaction or resolve an issue. Your team should have visibility to every interaction that has occurred across all channels with the customer up to that "moment of truth." The data they need should be at their fingertips not only to respond to the specific request, but also to anticipate their potential future needs based on interactions with other similar customers. Tools like Weaveability can greatly improve your team's ability to deliver a consistent, unified experience across all customer channels and touch points.

2. What are the channel preferences of your customers?
Customers have become accustomed to a retail society that is almost always open and accessible. With 24-hour stores and "always-on" social media, customers expect instant gratification. Social media interaction tools and online chat are enabling companies to be accessible at all hours and on their customers terms. Until recently, this technology was expensive and could only be afforded by companies with deep pockets. But that is no longer true. Today, even small retailers with limited budgets can leverage these capabilities for their own business.

Of course, many of your customers will still seek out more tangible, conversational interactions—preferring natural voice over text. Chatbots, using embedded natural language processing, are maturing rapidly. We predict they will become a standard way for companies to reduce friction in customer experiences and to eliminate long queues in their call centers. Chatbots are especially ideal for responding to customers who are asking routine or frequently asked questions. As a side benefit, this enables the company to focus their human CSRs on serving those customers with more challenging or complicated issues.

We can learn much from Staples as they evolve and enhance their omni-channel customer experience. Clearly, it is a company whose leaders have embraced a transformative approach to their business and they've tackled the 3S's. They have a simple and compelling Story, a clear and integrated go-to-market Strategy, and they are aligning their Systems (people, process, and technology) to deliver a remarkable, omni-channel customer experience.

Chapter 13

Making Innovation Real

bradyservices.com

"We are transforming from a building services company that uses technology to a technology company that is disrupting the building services sector."

—Jim Brady, President of Brady Services

Oftentimes, the most visionary and transformational leaders come from industries that are perceived by many to be the backwaters of innovation. Jim Brady is one such leader.

From humble beginnings 55 years ago, Brady has certainly come a long way. The heating, ventilation and air conditioning (HVAC) services company was founded by Jim's father, Don Brady, as a Trane HVAC franchise in Greensboro, North Carolina. Fast forward to today, and the Brady family of companies have emerged as innovators in smart buildings, smart cities and a category of innovative solutions broadly described as the "Internet of Things" (IoT). But this transformational journey has not been without its challenges.

When Jim first took the reins of the company from his father, he realized that he needed to gain a fuller understanding of their current brand positioning in the marketplace. If he was to reposition the company successfully as a technology innovator in the building services industry, he needed to deeply understand his customer and their needs and wants. The Brady brand had been so closely linked to the Trane HVAC brand for so many years that Jim knew that this shift would not be frictionless.

> *"Our company had been so successful for so many years that whenever talk of change came up, we always experienced huge pushback."*
>
> — Jim Brady

Jim's first hurdle was to overcome internal skepticism about the company's ability to execute a strategy positioning them as a technology innovator. How could Brady be considered an innovator when their own employees felt they lacked the requisite systems to support the existing business units? Brady had not sufficiently staffed skilled strategic marketing resources to build a leadership position based on an understanding of market needs.

Enter Harmandeep "Harman" Singh, the man who Jim tapped to help him formulate the strategy and make innovation real at Brady. Having played senior roles with Pacific Controls, Trane and Ingersoll Rand, Harman brought with him global knowledge and experience of marketing, sales and technology innovation in the building services industry.

Harman kicked things off by conducting over forty individual interviews of employees, customers and prospects to understand market perception of the current Brady brand and Jim's vision to become a technology leader. He then consolidated feedback to identify key marketing initiatives to drive brand understanding, development and execution. From this, he created a strategic "playbook" that detailed strategic initiatives to reposition the company as technology innovator and mobilize the team to make it happen.

> *"Innovation is literally at the center of our '3I' strategy: (Integrate, Innovate, Illuminate), which is not just about new technologies, it's more about our people."*
>
> — Harmandeep Singh, VP of Strategy and Innovation

One of the first plays was to recruit a group of innovators from across the company to begin driving transformation. Jim and Harman established the Brady Opportunity Launch Team ("BOLT") to work on diverse projects arising out of Brady's business needs or challenges. Using an agile ideation process, BOLT collects the ideas, quickly conducts experiments and builds a business case. Brady business unit leaders then decide when to activate the innovation in the core business. In this way, there is shared ownership and less disruption to the ongoing business.

Particularly impactful was establishing the Brady Innovation Center ("BIC"), located in the Brady corporate headquarters in Greensboro. Jim and Harman knew that gaining buy-in from customers and employees would be much easier if they could present a tangible and tactile experience of the destination they had planned for Brady. The BIC was outfitted with all of the latest technology and futuristic solutions for the building services industry. It quickly became the seat of new learning at the company, a laboratory for testing new ideas, and a show-case for modeling the future of Brady. In fact, Jim and Harman positioned the BIC as not a place to "see the future," but rather a place to "be the future."

From inspiration, illumination and integration in the BIC, the BOLT team has championed several new innovations for the company. For example, "Virtual Coach" enables senior Brady service technicians to remotely assist newer field technicians thereby delivering high quality outcomes for customers while not overextending senior resources.

"Virtual Energy Manager" allows Brady to monitor and manage the utility consumption of their customers remotely—making their customer look like a hero for reducing costs while increasing employee productivity.

"Building Clarity", their most ambitious entry in the "Smart Buildings" space, offers predictive and automated analytics to directly connect building perfor-mance to business results for Brady customers. Through innovations like these, and many more in the works, Brady expects to continue to grow, to change, and to use enabling technology to make their customers the hero by operating more comfortable, more productive and more profitable buildings.

Innovation Recognized

In 2017, Jim and his Brady Services team's efforts were recognized as the winner of the Most Innovative Workplace at the North Carolina Tech Awards. NC Tech Awards is North Carolina's only statewide technology awards program, recognizing companies and individuals who have characterized excellence, innovation and leadership.

> *"Since 1995, the NC Tech Awards has honored excellence and innovation throughout North Carolina, representing the best and the brightest. As a winner, Brady Services has distinguished itself as a peer-leader and we are proud to recognize them. "*
> — Brooks Raiford, president and CEO of NCTA

Transformational leaders like Jim Brady and Harman Singh understand the critical nature of having the conditions for success in place before embarking on a marketing transformation journey. Along the way, teams often get caught up with the tactical execution and fail to see the forest for the trees. Here are a few tips and takeaways from the Brady experience to help marketing leaders navigate transformation:

1. **Don't let the tactical distract from strategic business outcomes**
   The activities of sales and marketing are, by their very nature, tactical. When implementing a new technology or automation system, it's important to understand the business goals upfront. This will prevent operations from consuming unnecessary amounts of time and money. You need to challenge your thinking constantly by answering these strategic questions:
   - How do these tasks tie back to our overarching strategy?
   - What's our goal for this tactic?
   - Does that goal align with our strategy?

   If you can't clearly and succinctly answer these questions—it's time to rethink priorities and reallocate resources.

2. **Build an agile team that can respond when demand rises**
Solving for capacity starts with visibility. By creating a clear view of your teams' capacity, you are enabled to shift resources internally to meet changing demands. Also by creating a clear view, you are able to understand where there may be any potential skill gaps. This can be very helpful when you are trying to accurately determine which tasks need to be outsourced. Many companies are exploring the benefits of "Marketing-as-a-Service" to meet the ever-growing needs of sales, marketing and innovation.

"We had to balance the needs of innovating for the future while running a current profitable business. Establishing BOLT, using an agile approach and securing a marketing-as-a-service partner was critical to our success."
—Jim Brady, President Brady Services

With customers moving fast and technology moving faster (there are now more than 5,000 marketing technology solutions), it is critical for CMOs to adopt an agile mindset and inspire their teams to be innovative, risk-takers, authentic, inclusive, and athletic because, often, needed functions have yet to be designed.

3. **Define your key performance indicators (KPIs) based on business objectives**
In order to stay focused on the KPIs that tie back to strategic business goals, marketing teams must identify and track leading indicators and outcome-oriented measurements that matter. All marketing spend on media and asset creation should be visible. If campaign outcomes are unclear, your team needs to have a framework in place for making trade-offs. There should never be any "black holes" in your budget.

"Be clear about what business outcomes you are driving during transition. Don't just spend more; that's why CMOs get fired. Only sign up for budget if you can deliver revenue for it."
— Kristin Lemkau, CMO, JP Morgan Chase

4. Get aligned internally and break down marketing silos
   Authenticity starts with your brand story and mission, and change is driven from the inside out. Therefore, marketing must first get aligned internally. By having an aligned team and a more transparent structure, organizations can eliminate duplicate tasks and reinvest the time, money, and effort in activities that drive the most ROI.

> *"Everything from the way we market and the way we interact internally and with our stakeholders to the way we innovate and the talent we develop and find must be connected to those core values to become the brand we aspired to be. Otherwise, the authenticity is just not there, and that will completely undermine credibility."*
> — Rob Lynch, CMO, Arby's

Don't forget, alignment of stakeholders is key to implementing a new marketing technology — do not under-estimate the power of a decision-maker who gets left out of the planning process.

5. **Don't get caught up in the marketing transformation mayhem**
   While you may not have spaghetti plot charts revealing where the marketing mayhem will come from this week, you can feel confident that it's headed your way. In order to navigate the unruly waters of marketing transformation, you'll have to proactively develop a strategic playbook and ensure the conditions of success are in place.

By having the conditions for success in place, your team can successfully run transformational plays and navigate the pitfalls. If you recognize the common signs of marketing mayhem, you can take proactive measures to prevent the chaos from getting out of control. If you're looking for more information about managing through transformational mayhem, read on! We'll go into far greater detail the next section of the book!

The Brady story teaches us that making innovation real requires a new mindset and a different blend of skills. It begins with a deep and specific understanding of the customer, i.e., what the customer wants and needs at every stage of their decision-making journey.

Transformative leaders like Jim Brady invest in understanding the entire customer experience much better than their peers. They also have much better processes for capturing insights about customers and applying these insights to their marketing programs.

As we have noted in previous chapters, **instead of focusing on the greatness of a company's products and services, an innovative brand makes their customer the hero.** Real innovation comes when you interrupt marketing as usual and formulate a compelling strategy to tell a simple, clear and aligned brand story to the right person, at the right time, through the proper channel.

SYSTEMS

Chapter 14

Aligning Marketing Systems to Execute Strategy

Disney and Starbucks… What do these two companies have in common? Despite operating in different industries, their business models have many similarities: laser-focus on customer needs and wants; personalization of offers and messages; rigorous measurement and optimization of marketing. Both of these brands consider service excellence as a critical enabler of their growth strategy, and accordingly, they have mastered the art and science of customer experience management.

Starbucks's move to put Systems at the heart of the brand is paying off as revenues grew dramatically in 2016, up over 18 percent in the fourth quarter alone to $4.9 billion. The brand has aggressive plans to roll out even more innovative digital features in the near future like "mobile order and pay" which has been a huge hit with customers and has streamlined their coffee drinking experience.

"We've added this capability that provides significant convenience to the consumer, but we've done it in a way that does not take away from or prevent the full Starbucks experience. And thus far, I think we're seeing great results, great reception, and we're very confident that we're on the right path"
— Howard Schultz, CEO, Starbucks

Likewise, Disney has rolled out innovative, new technology to enable fun, relaxing, or inspiring experiences. The new "Magic Bands" are wearable devices that provide over 30 million guests a "friction free" and personalized experience at their Orlando theme parks, hotels, and resorts.

Of course, Disney and Starbucks are not the only companies that focus on creating compelling customer experiences (CX). In 2017, 89% of marketers expected customer experience to be their primary differentiator. Despite perceiving customer experience as a critical factor to generate sustainable growth and expecting it to become their differentiator, researchers have shown that less than 25% of companies excel on generating memorable experiences.

Many companies' definitions of customer experience are incomplete and they don't have the necessary tools in place to approach, design, and manage the full customer experience. Moreover, many marketers still confuse the concepts of customer experience and customer service. The reality is that the scope of customer experience extends far beyond the traditional definition of customer service—that is, the transactional moments when employees are providing direct service to customers.

So, what's going on?

You've got a great brand story—a simple, yet remarkable story.

You've formulated your go-to-market strategy—a clear path to reaching your target customers with the right message, through the right channel, at just the right time to get them to act.

Now, all that's missing to transform your marketing is the alignment of the needed Systems to scale and deliver measurable business results. Marketing

Systems enable you to flawlessly execute your strategy and measure the return on your marketing investment.

To be clear here, when we say "Systems" it means much more than just technology. Systems include the business processes, measurement systems, and organizational capabilities required to deliver, track, and manage the customer experience across every customer touchpoint: from the earliest stages of the BuyWay through to the empowerment of advocates and brand evangelists.

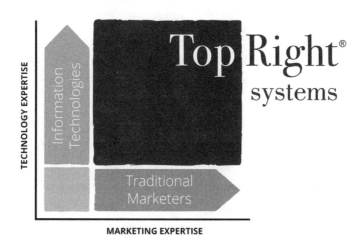

The best strategies are only as effective as their tactical execution. TopRight performing companies define and align their business processes, organizational structure, performance measures, marketing technology and change management required to efficiently operationalize the strategy, flawlessly deliver the customer experience and consistently measure the business results.

From a business process perspective in many companies, marketing still functions in a silo, separate from nearly every other financial decision made in the company. Company leaders—who agonize over whether to build a factory to fill additional capacity, whether to make that next technology upgrade, or even whether to acquire another company—routinely make marketing decisions that appear as if they've left their spreadsheets at home. **Marketing is an investment, pure and simple, not an optional expense or a luxury.** The processes that surround executing and tracking a marketing program should mirror the same processes that are put in place to ensure that every investment earns the neces-sary return.

This level of discipline doesn't exist in most marketing departments today. Many marketers claim that measuring results on tactics—from an advertising campaign to sponsoring an event—is too difficult or not worth the effort, as if this were akin to learning a foreign language. It's not surprising that marketing has earned a reputation as big spenders who take no financial responsibility.

Customer insights drive brand decision-making and marketing investments. The term "investment"—rather than expense—connotes the way marketing should function. Just as you should think twice before you pour your 401(k) funds into high-risk tech stocks or your neighbor's latest startup idea, so, too, should you think carefully before you gamble your marketing budget on a risky bet, especially when you likely have better options.

Creatively minded marketers shouldn't let all this "science" and "investment" talk overwhelm them. The art of marketing is now more important than ever. The creative genius that drives brilliant marketing remains a critical part of every-thing that a marketer does. But the left-brain aspects of marketing—investment management and other fact-based processes—can be enabled and strengthened by marketing technology. Furthermore, new marketing technology (MarTech) applications can give marketers the freedom to focus on brilliant creative ideas to deliver on strategy. The marketing investment approach, combined with creative drive, gives marketers an even greater ability to build their brand and drive value for their company. This is the Systems part of Transformational Marketing.

The brand and its Story stand at the center of everything that marketing does.

The TopRight transformational approach to marketing indicates that the way to evaluate a brand is based on how much it sells, not on the kind of finger-to-the-wind approach that might show up on the front page of Ad Age. Brands are only valuable as long as they sell—ask Smith-Corona what they think of the value of branding in and of itself.

Microsoft is a great brand, not because of some intrinsic value, but because Microsoft sells an awful lot of software.

Everyone's favorite example, Apple, is a great brand that excels at telling a great story, starting with, and being true to, its "why." And, it's one of the most profitable company in the world.

Customer insights that drive decision-making must be both relevant and timely.

Compiling such information is an enormous burden for nearly every company on the planet, but it's a necessary one.

In addition to poor internal processes and measurement systems, marketing also faces obstacles in the form of departmental silos. These enterprise constructs force companies to think about actions from the standpoint of operations or sales, rather than from the standpoint of the customer.

The construct of a functional silo is completely counter to the TopRight principles of simplicity, clarity and alignment. Silos create complexity for customers as the onus is on them to navigate disparate marketing, sales, finance and service channels.

Governance and decision-making across functional silos can be unclear and confusing for both employees and customers. And consistent delivery of your Story and execution of your Strategy can easily become misaligned as handoffs occur from silo-to-silo.

The 1990s era of corporate restructuring, exemplified in Champy and Hammer's *Reengineering the Corporation,* brought down many of these silos. At the time, many companies decided that it was a good time "not to automate, but to obliterate" old ways of doing things. Unfortunately, these restructuring projects rethought processes for almost all sections of the company *except* marketing.

Every other department has been reengineered and enabled by information technology. For too long, marketers have suffered behind the unseen walls that exist between marketing and all the other departments of the company. How can a company develop a remarkable customer experience for its customers that encompasses traditional selling and marketing activities as well as operations and services when it's almost impossible to get marketing and sales to speak with one another?

"Don't automate, obliterate."

— Dr. Michael Hammer

It is time for marketing organizations, and everything that makes them run, to be transformed from the inside out. Implementing a transformational approach to marketing cannot be accomplished with just a sheaf of studies or brainstorming. You have to put real changes in place that bring together organizational design, culture, incentives, processes, and marketing technology to make building and retaining a profitable customer relationship possible.

Financial discipline and scientific rigor must be involved in every marketing decision.

Otherwise, you'll stay stuck in the past, gambling away your marketing dollars.

Sales and marketing technologies have evolved significantly in the past few years and solutions like Customer Relationship Management (CRM), Digital Asset Management (DAM), Multi-Channel Campaign Management (MCCM), Marketing Resource Management (MRM), Marketing Performance Management (MPM) and Marketing Automation Platforms (MAP) have now matured to the point that they offer marketers a robust set of capabilities for managing their marketing with the intentionality and strategic discipline of TopRight companies.

The MarTech category of software applications is absolutely booming! As evidenced by the expanding marketing technology landscape updated each year by ChiefMarTec.com CEO Scott Brinker, picking the right "marketing stack" for your business is more akin to finding a needle in a haystack. Adoption is now easier than ever since the vast majority of MarTech solutions are available in the "Marketing Cloud," so barriers to entry are low for businesses of all sizes.

There's a lot of marketing technology in the world my friend…

Unfortunately, early adopters and many companies fail to realize the full benefits and potential of technologies in the Marketing Cloud. Like the famous line from the movie Field of Dreams, many software vendors promise you that "If you build it, [they] will come"—implying that the software possesses some mystical power to attract customers to your brand. "Field of Dreams" marketing ideas such as this never pay off. This false sense of trust in marketing technology is fundamental to many failures.

Ironically, many firms have embraced a new mantra of "customer-centricity" and implementing MarTech has been at the heart of their strategy. We encourage marketers to embrace these new technologies, but also caution them to understand that technologies are nothing more than enablers for marketing transformation.

> *"Software is modern marketing's middleman."*
> Scott Brinker, CEO, Chiefmartec.com

In and of itself, MarTech will not give you a new brand story, develop a winning strategy, or get more customers to buy your products and services. Market leaders use MarTech as a tool for gathering data about their customer personas, their journeys, and transactional behaviors. In turn, this data can be analyzed to reveal insight about trends in customer purchase behavior, to facilitate segmentation of the customer base, and to create customer preference for the brand over time.

MarTech can be an amazing set of tools for supporting brand-building activities. But more importantly, it can serve as a scientific decision support system for making the right investments, in the right amounts, at the right times to optimize overall returns on marketing investment for the company.

Transformational Marketing is about optimizing and mobilizing all marketing assets to create lasting preference for the brand, to activate customer purchase intent, and to accelerate organic growth of revenues and profits. To truly transform, marketing must get all 3S's right: the right Story, the right Strategy, and the right Systems, all measured through the lens of Simplicity, Clarity and Alignment.

Move your brand to the TopRight corner of the markets where you compete

These are a lot of barriers to address, it's true. It's not easy work to make the marketing in your company function the way it's supposed to: driving sales. But, it's possible and the rewards are significant.

To move to the top right corner of performance, you must unleash the true power of your brand and interrupt "marketing as usual" techniques. Apply science and art to your marketing efforts, and you can create productive conversations to engage your customer. Engage your customer and convert them into advocates, and you can drive your revenues and profits ever higher. You have to develop a deep understanding—backed by some real scientific rigor and creative magic—of your market and your customers. Only then can you powerfully develop your brand's story, strategy and enabling systems to communicate efficiently and effectively with your target audience, identifying different customer personas and tailoring your messages appropriately at every touch-point in their buying journey.

To help you along the way, here are fourteen transformational tips to help you bring simplicity, clarity, and alignment to your Marketing Systems:

1. Use dashboards for visibility into capacity and workflows.
2. Understand your KPIs. Do they align with your strategy? Be upfront with the metrics that are going to matter and hold your team accountable to hit those.
3. Measure for ROI on everything, including processes.

4. Establish both a database that provides visibility into marketing performance as well as processes that make it easy to capture the data needed to measure ROI accurately.

5. Be ruthlessly consistent that everything in your budget aligns with your strategic marketing plan.

6. Show your finance team the research that's led to your budgetary requests and then prove that they can trust you.

7. Be visible with your spending. Hold your team and others accountable for what they spend and always have a solid answer for "How, where, and when did you allocate your budget?"

8. Set up processes that enable visibility.

9. Measure the impact of marketing throughout the customer's lifecycle.

10. Generate executive-level performance reports in the "language of the business" (ROI) to reinforce accountability in action.

11. Manage your assets with a "single version of the truth." Consider a digital asset management (DAM) tool that allows you to easily store, organize, track and repurpose your branded assets (such as photography, videos, rich graphics, 3D imagery, text documents, PowerPoint presentations) resulting in greater brand and licensing compliance and increased team productivity and efficiency.

12. Communication between partners is key. Metrics, processes, opportunities should all be communicated constantly.

13. For your distribution partners, get in the habit of sharing data. Meet regularly to review important data points so that you can leverage your collective knowledge to understand customers better.

14. Enable a "learn-act-learn" culture where risk-taking in the marketplace is not only tolerated but encouraged.

All of your marketing, all employee communications, all sales collateral, all enabling technologies, all of your people at every customer touchpoint must be fully aligned to bring your brand to life. **Alignment equates to the "how."** How do your people communicate your story? How do you want your customers to experience your brand? And how do you specifically deliver value?

This is often where companies and organizations struggle the most.

Your ultimate goal is to align your marketing systems to execute your strategy with ruthless consistency. Of course, managing your marketing team's capacity is only going to get more difficult as customer demands and marketing channels increase.

If you have internal visibility into capacity and processes, you can manage your marketing team more easily. With clear visibility, you can start to find the pain points in your processes, and you can address them appropriately.

With the right marketing systems in place you can identify the impediments that are hamstringing your sales and marketing talent, obscuring your brand story or damaging the customer experience.

Chapter 15

Selecting the Right Partner Not the Next Bright Shiny Object

flic.kr/p/YWWEnB

Marketers love chasing the latest and greatest "bright shiny object" [BSO] and there are plenty of them out there. Almost every day, we're inundated with new cloud-based marketing automation platforms, social media networks, or mobile messaging apps with the promise to skyrocket brand share, influence, and sales. As a transformative marketer, it's always important to keep up with the latest new thing, right?

Not necessarily.

Before grabbing onto the latest BSO or "disruptive technology", it's important to remember that business results come first. The first point of consideration is whether this new tool or trend will enable you to achieve those business results, closely followed by how it will achieve those results.

After all, the value is in what the BSO delivers, not the BSO itself.

The opportunity cost of perpetually chasing the next BSO disrupts and distracts from other important priorities, which are pushed aside to make room for the next new thing.

There's no doubt that marketing needs to take risks. The distinction here is that the most successful brands and companies **are more deliberate and intentional when it comes to assessing new marketing opportunities and new technologies as they emerge.**

If I told you how many new marketing technology products and services were released this past year, it would shock you. Literally thousands of new offerings were launched in the US alone. Most of these products and services will go nowhere, even if they start out going somewhere. Consider this example.

In early 2016, the co-founder of Vine launched a new iPhone social media app called Peach. Peach offers a mash-up of functionality from many familiar apps like Facebook, Twitter, Slack, Snapchat and Instagram all rolled into one. The Peach brand story is pretty simple: "Life is filled with words, pictures, places, and songs worth sharing and when you put these things together, expressing yourself is faster, easier, and more fun."

But their strategy is pretty unclear. Who is the target audience and what's the compelling reason for them to roll all of their social interactions into one place? And the competition in this space is fierce. Twitter, SnapChat and Instagram are so culturally entrenched that they've entered our vocabulary as concepts in and of themselves—we think in tweets, snaps, and instagrams.

The launch of Peach triggered a huge response as it debuted near the top of Apple's iPhone download list. Then, four days after its meteoric launch, the tech pundits declared that the "Peach is rotten" as downloads plummeted. If you had invested time and money in engaging with Peach, you would be left today with nothing but a pit in your stomach.

You don't have to treat trends like a day at the horse races. Transformative marketers should not be so quick to move with the trends. Successful marketing requires focus, sustained energy and commitment. The opportunity cost of perpetually chasing the next BSO disrupts and distracts from other important priorities. Transformative marketers must be extremely intentional when it comes to assessing new marketing opportunities and new technologies as they emerge. Here is a directed approach for picking the right horse in a crowded field.

Question the need for that BSO. Don't just take off after the new trend because everyone else is. Instead, take a deep look at why this trend has appeal and whether it's absolutely necessary for your success.

You must be sure to articulate your Brand Destination, which specifies how you want the customer to think, feel and act about your brand. More importantly it quantifies the results you expect your company to generate in the marketplace. A clear brand destination provides a lens through which you evaluate BSO's and make the right marketing decisions to achieve success—giving marketing leaders a constructive way to say "no" to chasing the next shiny object.

Define metrics for success. Before following any trend and implementing any approach, it's crucial to know how success will be measured. Use CLEAR (Collaborative, Limited, Emotional, Appreciable, and Refinable) goals as a means of tracking marketing performance and navigating the brand to its destination. It's extremely important to not only specify what success looks like when you arrive at the Destination, but also what it looks like at milestones along the way. Any BSO must be assessed in the context of your Brand Destination and the CLEAR goals you are committed to achieving--otherwise they are nothing more than distractions and resource drains."

Consider the Hype Cycle. The general pattern of trends is predictably unpredictable pattern. The premise of the hype cycle is that people tend to get overexcited about new shiny objects, and then they are disappointed when the shiny objects don't change the world in the blink of an eye. That said, some of the shiny objects do actually change the world, given the right market conditions and some patience. For marketers, this is where things actually get interesting. If the BSO promises to get you to your Brand Destination faster and achieve your CLEAR goals, it may be worthy of further investigation and experimentation.

Re-calibrate marketing priorities. You shouldn't spend resources you don't have or commit to more than you can afford to risk. Marketing budgets and resources aren't unlimited. Therefore, if you do decide that a BSO is worth chasing, then something has to drop off your marketing plate to take on something new. Marketing priorities will have to be re-calibrated, CLEAR goals realigned and any dependencies or conflicts with other marketing programs must be reconciled.

Investigate and experiment. If your marketing team is truly serious about pursuing a new trend, then you must commit sufficient resources to evaluate the situation. Establish a small team and test the ideas that show the most promise for building your brand and growing your business with the trend. If something shows potential, then you can expand it and incorporate it into your overall marketing mix and adjust your CLEAR goals accordingly.

Learn from failure. Sometimes companies invest resources in following the trend, only to find that despite their best efforts, it was nothing but a red herring. Sadly, failure will happen, but it also provides valuable learning if those lessons are applied during the next go-round.

You can't underestimate the importance of building a learning culture with all of your employees to improve the process along the way. Build a culture that rewards learning fast and failing fast. Hire people who exhibit intellectual curiosity and recognize them for it. Ultimately that's always the best trend to follow.

One of my bosses early in my career used to publicly proclaim, "Stop complaining—all marketers are resource constrained—you just need to learn how to do more with less!"

At the time, I took issue with this sweeping generalization. However, since the most recent recession, I have found a great deal of truth in that statement.

Perhaps this is one of the reasons why the field of Marketing Automation (MA) has become white-hot in the past five years. MA is a category of technology that allows companies to streamline, automate, and measure marketing tasks and work-flows, so marketers can increase operational efficiency and grow revenue faster.

These days it seems that every major software company is staking their claim and proclaiming their leadership position in MA. Unfortunately for the market-ers tasked with finding the right solution, there appears to be widespread confu-sion on which vendors lead the pack, even among industry analyst firms (e.g. Forrester, Gartner, etc.)

So, here are ten critical considerations for selecting the right Marketing Systems partner:

1. Ensure you receive phone support—you will need it. Find out what other forms of support are available and the hours of operation.

2. Find out if training on the software is included with your purchase. If not, how much does it cost?

3. Be sure the software integrates with your current CRM solution and data can flow freely between the two platforms. See if it integrates with other platforms you use-a single view of all contact information is valuable.

4. If you are changing MA vendors, make sure the vendor has successfully migrated data from your current platform to their software. Find out how difficult this is and what it entails. Is technical expertise needed?

5. Find out how pricing scales, especially regarding database size. Are there add-on features available or do you have to upgrade for more features or additional contacts? You need to know the true cost of the platform before purchasing. Are there hidden fees? Limits of messages sent a month? Charges to add users?

6. Find out if the software is designed for use by both sales and marketing. How it will better align sales and marketing teams? Ask for examples of how each team can use it.

7. Does the platform manage full customer life cycles, or only leads and prospects? You want to be able to engage and nurture contacts through-out the entire life cycle. After all, the best customer you can get is the one you already have.

8. Ask about email deliverability, specifically the vendor's inbox and deliver-ability rate. This is an oft-overlooked but incredibly important aspect to a successful MA platform.

9. Metrics and reporting vary greatly between vendors. What metrics are available to track campaign performance? Also, be sure to find out how the software measures/defines success. What metrics does the dashboard emphasize? Are reports customizable?

10. Ensure the software offers mobile optimized landing pages and forms, as well as responsive email templates. Do you have additional mobile technology needs? It is essential that the software can meet your mobile requirements.

In order to be successful with marketing systems (and long before you select a vendor technology), you have to create your go-to-market strategy and empower the people who will actually own the success of not just the marketing platforms, but also of the entire demand generation process. Someone must be accountable to deliver on the metrics (number of qualified leads, conversion rates, cost per lead, etc.), as well as someone who will own the process and enabling technology platform. In many small companies, it's the same person. In larger companies, it's not.

As Michael Hammer so wisely said in his now famous HBR Article (*"Reengineering Work: Don't Automate, Obliterate"*, HBR, July-August 1990), "It is time to stop paving the cow paths. Instead of embedding outdated processes in silicon and software, we should obliterate them and start over. We should reengineer our businesses: use the power of modern information technology to radically redesign our business processes in order to achieve dramatic improvements in their performance."

So, if you're a marketer struggling to do more with less and you want to move to the TopRight corner of the markets where you compete, don't just chase after the next BSO. Refer back to your brand destination statement and then select the right partner who will help align your people, processes and platforms to execute your strategy and tell your brand story in the most efficient and effective way to drive growth.

Chapter 16

Exposing the Little White Lies About Marketing Automation

Do you remember the story about a happy customer named Jeaneth Manzaniita Tavares who posted a raving review about her pizza on the Domino's Facebook page?

> *"Best Pizza Ever! Pan Pizza :) Keep up the good work guys!"*
>
> Customer

Mistakenly, an automated bot programmed by the company to deal with complaints replied:

> *"So sorry about that! Please share some additional information with us at [link] and please mention reference #1409193 so we can have this addressed."*
>
> Domino's Pizza

Oops! Attempting to use a little sarcastic humor to patch things up, Domino's tried to cover its tracks:

"No, we meant we were sorry it took Jeaneth so long to enjoy the best pizza ever. Think of all the pizza she's likely had that wasn't the best ever!"

Domino's Pizza

Social media lit up. Agitated customers lashed out at Domino's and chastised them for the use of impersonal, inauthentic, automated bots for handling their social media interactions. It turns out that the social media savvy possess no patience for dishonesty. If you find your brand in this situation, it is always best to just apologize, own the problem and fix it as quickly as possible. Afterall, marketers are humans. We make mistakes. And so do the marketing systems that we rely on to tell our brand stories and execute our strategies! So, you can't just "set it and forget it!"

The Dangers of "Going Viral"

Transformational marketers know that if you want to accelerate sales, putting the right digital marketing systems in place is crucial to executing and scaling your strategy.

Crafting an automated marketing campaign with compelling content and powerful imagery is one of the most effective ways to attract new customers, but social media doesn't come without a fair degree of risk. In fact, you can just as easily put yourself out of business by forgetting how quickly news can spread via social media.

Sounds like a good problem, right?

Timothy's Coffees of the World did what many brands have done to increase sales—they setup an automated marketing campaign that offered a free sample to customers for following them on social.

Unfortunately, Timothy's offered more than they could deliver. For "liking" Timothy's on Facebook, the company offered to send fans four free 24-pack boxes of Keurig single cup coffees.

Unsurprisingly, customers were ecstatic and snapped up the offer—depleting the company's supply of free K-cup packs after only three days. Two weeks later, the company's marketing team sent out a message to customers saying the offer was "first come first serve." Talk about too little too late.

Despite an apology video and distribution of free coupons in the mail, Timothy's is still trying to recover from the fan backlash on social media. When it comes to social media, companies often focus on quantity (how many likes/followers/retweets) without thinking about why and how they plan to engage the customer after.

Your marketing systems not only should help you scale and execute your Strategy, but they must also be true to your Brand Story and align the inherent promises that it makes to customers.

Hopefully, you'll never find yourself in one of these precarious situations with your brand. But just in case, learn more about how you can avoid these types of mistakes and take control of the ensuing mayhem by taking a transformational approach to marketing.

The Little White Lies

In a 2015 report, the top three complaints from marketers were the software takes too long to implement, is too expensive and too risky. Sound familiar?

While Marketing Automation Platforms open up new frontiers, the little white lies that vendors employ to make the sale—and that we believe—are an expensive source of confusion.

Success in marketing automation goes far beyond just choosing the right vendor.

To help clear the air, here are nine little white lies about MAP'S:

1. **Implementing a MAP is "set it and forget it"**

   The term marketing *automation* is a little misleading and while it is true that you set up a campaign and it "runs" automatically, it isn't that simple. Any marketing technology you implement requires dedicated human interaction to be successful. No MAP will analyze the page views vs opt-ins vs qualified leads and adjust the campaign accordingly, or monitor which email sequence converts the best and explain why.

   Once sales identify a new bottleneck, who is going to generate the new content to drive leads to complete the opt-in form? Who is going to generate content to re-engage older leads, especially if your company has a longer sales cycle? Who is going to adjust the email subject line if no one is opening your emails? Be wary if your MAP Vendor alludes to a "set it and forget it" approach, as it just isn't true.

2. **Marketing Automation will save you boatloads of time**

   Do not be fooled by this statement.

   Unless you are performing every single task a MAP can perform on a daily basis—and trust me, you aren't—it won't save you time.

   "It takes longer every year!"

   — Scott Brinker
   VP Platform Ecosystem at Hubspot

   Getting a MAP up and running is not a quick and easy task. Choosing and making the move to Marketing Automation requires buy-in from all stakeholders. Prior to launching your first campaign, your team will put dozens of hours into buyer personas, data analysis, campaign design, copywriting (landing page, email, social media, paid ads), email sequences, and data configuration to personalize and segment messages. Don't forget the alignment of your sales/marketing systems and processes—a difficult piece of the puzzle for many organizations.

3. **All it takes is a team of one**

C-suite execs and MAP Vendors are equally guilty of perpetuating this lie. Getting C-suite buy-in for new software is hard and MAP Vendors use statements like, "We make our software so easy a 12-year old can setup a campaign" or "It only takes 5 hours a week to manage" to help expedite the C-suite buy-in. Unfortunately, what often happens is the company doesn't have the proper resources in place to correctly execute the setup, management, analytics, and A/B testing necessary to make marketing automation pay off in the long run.

MAP's are multi-channel, involve different segments, engage sales and marketing, and activate prospects at different points in the funnel. Marketing Automation should touch every part of your organization—customer support, sales, lead generation, lead cultivation, marketing, recruiting, after-sales, etc. It isn't something that can be added to your VP Marketing's to-do list. It requires dedicated focus and special skills.

4. **You need to hire a MAP rock star with tons of experience to ensure success**

Looking for a rock star with 5-10 years of MAP experience may not be your best bet. Platforms have changed, technologies have changed, and there are dozens of new channels to engage prospects. You need to find someone who understands your brand voice, buyer personas, and culture; who has experience launching and managing the technical and creative aspects of personalized marketing and/or email automation campaigns; who knows the channels in which to reach your target market. In today's Marketing Automation world, you need someone who knows conversion and understands the value of a real lead.

5. **Marketing Automation doesn't require any technical skills**

Has your marketing team segmented email lists by event details and/or user attributes? Do they know how to correctly configure what attributes need to be sent to the MAP—and how to map that information? Do they have experience with domain configuration, email authentication, DNS, and A/B testing? How is personalization added to your marketing messages?

In 2015, it was reported by Gartner that only 38% of those that have MA use advanced tactics like progressive profiling. Progressive profiling requires a technical understanding of how data is gathered and how to best segment this information. You are seriously limiting the potential of your platform's ROI by overlooking the technical skills necessary to successfully execute a lead generation program.

Beyond the technical skills, an understanding and experience in email deliverability, email list best practices, and reengaging old leads are valuable assets to keep your emails out of the spam folder.

6. **The more I pay for a platform, the more likely my emails are to reach the inbox**

When was the last time you asked a MAP vendor for their email deliverability rate and statistics while researching platforms? Did you, like most marketers, assume that was just "part of the package"? After all, the hefty price tag should guarantee email deliverability, right? Wrong. One of the most overlooked considerations for a MAP vendor is email deliverability rate and email list policies.

Marketing Automation is complex enough, and the nitty gritty details of email deliverability are rarely covered in the sales process—specifically, that it's the marketer's job to follow email best practices, only send email to opted-in contacts, and remove invalid email addresses proactively. Talk to your vendor about this up-front to avoid serious deliverability issues that can wreak havoc on your lead generation program.

7. **It's just an email marketing platform with some fancy features**

Don't confuse an email service provider (ESP) with a MAP. While ESPs like Constant Contact and Customer.io have entered the automation field with some fancy features, they are lacking major functions of a robust MAP. For example, MAP vendors offer a unified customer view, multi-channel functionality, buyer persona mapping, landing pages and forms, lead scoring, sales/marketing integration, and can even go beyond the digital realm to trigger direct mail pieces based on actions performed by users.

8. **The vendor with the best publicity is clearly the top choice**
MAP vendors are not one-size fits all, and it is not a decision to be made lightly. Your systems and technology must match your business needs. It's important to understand fully what you are purchasing and ensure that it is the right platform for your specific business needs. It should be aligned with your overall sales and marketing strategy, and you should secure the necessary resources prior to adopting and launching a new MAP vendor. As you navigate through the thousands of articles comparing vendors, remember, you are reading marketing by other marketers.

9. **Implementing a MAP will automatically generate tons of qualified leads**
Implementing a MAP will generate leads, but if your content isn't aligned with your buyer personas/target market segments/target accounts—or if these are completely inaccurate—the leads aren't going to be qualified. You first have to understand your audience and speak to them in a way that compels them to engage with your brand. If anything, an unsuccessful Marketing Automation campaign may reveal if the audience you think you are targeting is indeed the audience engaging with your brand.

In summary, implementing a Marketing System takes lots of work, consumes time (and more every year), requires teamwork, and ongoing support.

"Martech is going mainstream. By now, everyone has had a CMS and a CRM. But in terms of other marketing technologies—whether it's personalization, content marketing or social media management software—we've crossed the chasm from Early Adopters to now the Early and Late Majority. Executives at "Main Street" companies are now acknowledging the need to adopt these tools."
— Scott Brinker
VP Platform Ecosystem at Hubspot

There are plenty of other marketing automation myths: it's cold and imper-sonal, businesses with long sales cycle aren't ideal candidates, and it doesn't work. You can probably come up with more. However, what's important to keep in mind is: *Marketing Automation is just a tool.*

Successful transformational marketing begins with a deep understanding—backed by some real scientific rigor and creative magic—of your market and your customers. Only then can you powerfully develop your Brand Story, Strategy and enabling Systems to create profitable, productive customer experiences.

9 LITTLE WHITE LIES
ABOUT **MARKETING AUTOMATION** PLATFORMS

1. Implementing a Marketing Automation Platform is "set it and forget it"

2. Marketing Automation Software will save you boatloads of times

3. All it takes is a team of one

4. You need to hire a Marketing Automation rockstar with tons of experience to ensure success

5. Marketing Automation doesn't require any technical skills

6. The more I pay for a platform, the more likely my emails are to reach the inbox

7. It's just an email marketing platform with some fancy features

8. The vendor with the best publicity is clearly the top choice

9. Implementing a Marketing Automation Platform will automatically generate tons of qualified leads

Chapter 17

Establishing the Conditions for Success

For anyone who has ever lived through a transformational project involving big change, you know that it can be a journey with many ups and downs. And not unlike riding "Kingda Ka" (at Six Flags Great Adventure in Jackson, New Jersey), it's either the ride of your life or the scariest thing you've ever done—or a little bit of both!

On the "King", you leave the station going from 0 to 128 miles per hour in a jaw-dropping 3.5 seconds. Actually, there isn't even be time for your jaw to drop. You shoot straight up that impossible height so fast, you don't even have time to think, so you just hang on. Arriving at the top, you immediately plummet right back down in a 270-degree spiral. There is very little that can prepare you for a drop of this intensity—most people just wing it.

Now, the beginning of your transformational marketing journey may not be quite as hair-raising, and your initial climb may not cause nose-bleeds, but based on our 10-years of experience, the first few moments will certainly set the tone for the rest of your journey. Furthermore, if you take the time to get a few things firmly in place before you're strapped in and leaving the station, it can make a world of difference in terms of your enjoyment of the ride. There is no need for you to wing it!

There's a reason this coaster is known as the "King." *Kingda Ka* is quite simply the tallest and fastest roller coaster in North America. This upside down U-shaped track bolts up 45 stories in the sky—that's 456 feet high! This leaves all other coasters in the dust. And of course, it's going to take some mighty acceleration to get you to the top of it!

The Transformational Marketing Journey and Productivity

After the commitment has been made to transform marketing, there is often a period of increased productivity and a level of anticipatory excitement —we sometimes refer to this as **"Uninformed Optimism."** Even though no real changes have been initiated yet, the marketing team actually performs at a slightly higher level in anticipation of the new capabilities that are coming.

Once the program is initiated and changes begin, a different and more complex phenomenon occurs. On an individual level, a new learning curve begins (and it may be a steep climb for some of your marketers). This is accompanied by a sharp decline in performance at the individual and team level (and perhaps at the business unit or company level depending on the scope and scale of the transformational initiative). We refer to this phenomenon of declining performance as the **"Valley of Despair."** The Valley is characterized by a steep fall in productivity, followed by a slow rise to previously established performance levels. The Valley of Despair is a natural organizational response to the major changes that frequently occur when change is implemented. Minimizing the depth and length of time that the organization spends in the trough of the "Valley" is critical to a successful marketing program implementation. We'll go into more detail on how to do this in the next section.

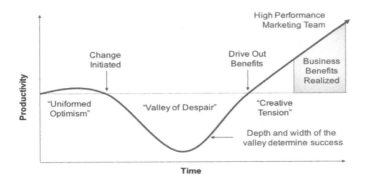

As the organization emerges from the Valley and overall marketing productivity rapidly increases, a new form of stress and tension will occur. Not unlike riding a roller coaster, people begin to speculate that there is another steep decline just over the next rise. The organization may again begin to feel the stress of the unknown and want to close their eyes and duck their heads. At this stage, it is important to note that not all tension and stress is bad. In fact, under the right circumstances, tension is essentially a structure that helps to facilitate creativity and increases people's ability to change.

You generate "**Creative Tension**" when you have a clarity about your desired brand destination and alignment on the "truth about today", (i.e. the gap is clear and people are motivated to change).

One's stake in marketing transformation determines one's level of stress

When it comes to roller coasters, everyone seems to be a little different. The "thrill seekers" have never seen a coaster they didn't love and they always clamor to sit in the first row. The "coaster phobics" avoid them at all costs.

There are a lot of people in the middle who aren't sure what they feel—until they're harnessed-in and asking themselves, "What was I thinking?" The best advice I ever received about riding roller coasters: keep your eyes open and look forward. Being able to see what is happening actually helps dispel **fear and nausea**.

With a better understanding of the entire transformational marketing journey up front, your eyes are now fully open and you're looking forward. However, there are still some things you must get in place before you strap in and leave the station. If you establish the conditions for success up front, you can navigate the stress points, avoid the pitfalls and generate the creative tension that will help catapult you to the next level of marketing performance.

Managing the Undercurrents of Marketing Transformation

If you've ever worked on a complex, far-reaching, transformational initiative for any period of time, you've probably experienced a project that felt like a complete disaster. The scope was out of control, deadlines routinely missed, campaigns sputtering, executives slashing resources, and team members at each other's throats. The undercurrents are strong and swift. And if you're not careful, it's easy to get pulled under or worse: pushed out the door.

> *"Everybody has a plan until they get punched in the mouth"*
> — Mike Tyson

Trust me, we've all been there.

According to a study in 2016 by PricewaterhouseCoopers, more than 60 percent of project failures are linked to internal issues such as insufficient resources or missed deadlines. In other words, failure is linked to common situations that a good project manager with a good project plan should be able to avoid.

Conversely, you probably can recall situations in which the environment surrounding a project was extremely positive, enabling success to be achieved in spite of serious shortcomings in the planning and management of project activities.

So, what's going on here?

How important is planning and project management in marketing transformation success?

The short answer: very important. However, there is more going on here than meets the eye. Just having a buttoned-up project plan, an agile methodology, and a great project manager does not guarantee success.

What is the real science behind planning for transformational marketing success?

We have identified five key activities that must be part of any project plan if transformational marketing success is to be achieved:

- **Quantifying Explicit Value**—There is a specific activity defined in the plan for quantifying and validating explicit value associated with the marketing project. The sponsoring executive and the project team have mutually agreed on a business case that is clearly defined and measurable in terms of strategic, operational, economic, and organizational benefit. These two parties have also agreed upon a case for user adoption at an individual level.

- **Generating Full Alignment**—There is a specific process defined for generating and sustaining executive alignment. The executive sponsor for the project and associated business leaders are well aligned on the priority of the marketing transformation effort and achievement of intended business outcomes. There is informed understanding and intention among all of the key stakeholders about the complete journey to results, and its many challenges and individual implications for employees in their roles.

- **Showcasing Sponsorship and Accountability in Action**—Specific activities are outlined in the plan to demonstrate how leadership is personally "at stake" and visible to the organization throughout the project. An executive leader or executive leadership team is in place with the positional authority, credibility, skill, resolve, and time to get the marketing transformation moving, and maintain its momentum through to results.

- **Securing Active Commitment**—There is a track of work for testing for active commitment regularly with leadership and the project team. Rooting out "passive" commitment to the project and/or passive aggressive behaviors regarding changes to marketing is imperative. Marketing leaders take personal responsibility for the program, take a stand for success, and are seen to take sides on conflicts and difficult issues.

- **Managing Performance Risk**—Activities are defined in the plan to assure that team performance is routinely monitored and risks are mitigated. Scope for the marketing team must be appropriate to obtain the business results desired; neither so broad nor so narrow as to jeopardize success. A performance evaluation process is in place to assure that the project is appropriately staffed with high-quality, high-performing talent—representing the cross-functional expertise needed to meet the business objectives.

It may come as somewhat of a surprise that these 5 key activities focus more on the management of people-related and culture-centered issues rather than process or technology focused concerns.

> *"The P in PM is as much about "people management" as it is about*
> *"project management""*
> — Cornelius Fichtner

A Word About Change Management

Change Management is the label we customarily give to the work activities applied to fostering the favorable work environment that is so vitally important to the ultimate outcome of marketing transformation.

However, there are two significant problems with this label. First, the label itself carries a connotation that is counterproductive at best. Change Management suggests an activity that is performed on the marketing organization (and hence is undiscussable) rather than a planned activity that is undertaken openly and cooperatively between the marketing executive sponsors, project team members, and the rest of the organization.

Second, the label is vague. There's nothing which even comes close to an objective and tangible definition. Depending on one's perspective, change may be "inevitable", change may be "painful", a little change may "do you good", or it may even be a "welcome change."

In accumulating years of experience managing large-scale marketing transformation work and the associated organizational change, the notion of "conditions for success" has emerged. This turns out to be an extremely important distinction in our thinking and our language for a couple of reasons.

First, "creating and sustaining the conditions for success" is something that a marketing leader or executive sponsor immediately identifies with as being very important to their own personal success. Hence, that which was undiscussable and unilateral as Change Management becomes highly discussable and collaborative.

Second, the "conditions for success" label is a more concrete definition that implies measurability and action-ability. The conditions for success are either in place or they are not. Therefore, a diagnostic can be defined to help measure the current state, to evaluate periodically throughout the project, and to prescribe specific actions to maintain the conditions for success.

If one or more of the conditions for success are not in place, you may get "lost in transformation." The "Valley of Despair" for your organization may be lengthy and deeply unproductive. If the conditions for success are ignored, a transformational marketing project may become stuck in the "Valley" requiring remediation to reinitiate the project. By diagnosing the conditions for success, you can surface the stress points, reveal symptoms and take action to minimize the depth and length of time that your organization spends in the "Valley." Some of the "how-to's" and prescriptive treatments include:

- Developing a <u>Case for Action</u> that links Marketing Transformation to Explicit Value

- Securing and Sustaining <u>Executive Alignment</u>

- Generating <u>Accountability in Action</u>

- Rooting out Passive Commitment and <u>Taking a Stand for Success</u>

- Managing the <u>Undercurrents of Marketing Transformation</u>

Now, as you strap in for your transformational marketing journey, eyes wide open and looking forward, you can breathe easy knowing that you have put the conditions for success in place.

While you're at it, don't forget to put your arms up and enjoy the ride. Simultaneous smiling and screaming is encouraged as you move to the TopRight corner of the markets where you compete!

Chapter 18

Not Getting Lost in Transformation

stock.adobe.com

A BC, the broadcast network which produced the hit television series "Lost", is part of the Disney–ABC Television Group. The ABC Entertainment Marketing department devises the marketing strategy and produces the promotional materials for all of the ABC television products for delivery to a variety of distribution channels. Steven Bushong, the SVP of Marketing Operations, is responsible for the effectiveness and efficiency of marketing operations with specific oversight on the development of marketing systems to execute the marketing strategy.

The marketing operations team was facing significant limitations in available information on marketing strategies for TV productions, the required marketing assets, marketing headcount, forecasted workload and performance measures. Under Steven's leadership, ABC planned to implement a new marketing production and operations management system ("PROMAS") to close the information gaps and streamline marketing production processes.

However, the project faced significant transformational headwinds. The demand for increased analytic rigor would have to co-exist in harmony within a highly artistic and creative culture. A classic left brain, right brain conflict was looming.

Steven kicked off the project by validating business requirements and workflows and mapping them to their selected marketing automation platform. He recognized that he must make explicit linkages to the strategy and its value for the Entertainment Marketing department. If the team did not clearly understand "what's in it for the business" he did not stand a chance. He also wanted the team to know that he would be very visible on the project because of its importance to the business. He encouraged accountability in action from the team and declared that he was "all-in" and committed to the success of the project.

It was also important to ensure there was complete team alignment before the first line of code would be touched. To facilitate this, Steven and the team created an illustrative marketing workflow. This came to life as a "hands-on lab" to engage marketing users directly in system design and configuration decisions. Based on lessons from past projects, he knew that people would support what they helped to create, so it was important to create a shared ownership of the project with the end users of the technologies.

The Result?

Truth be told, it was not a completely smooth ride. Many stress points were encountered along the way and tension on the project was not always in check. Conflicting priorities for resources on the project were a challenge and early results with the prototype were somewhat disappointing.

However, there were also welcome discoveries and breakthroughs. By striking a balance between the left brain and right brain talents, Steven was able to focus the tension on finding creative solutions and workarounds to seemingly intractable problems.

In the end, Steven successfully managed the undercurrents of transformation and generated significant results for the marketing operations. The team was able to endure the "valley of despair" and reach new levels of productivity by streamlining marketing production processes.

They are now managing over 13,000 marketing assets per year with over

7,000 of those being produced in-house. The new marketing systems also enable enhanced visibility between campaign management and the production workflows, allowing management to react more quickly to the dynamics of the business.

Identifying and Addressing the Stress Points

In the case of a transformational marketing project like ABC, one's personal stake in and perspective on marketing transformation actually determines one's level of anxiety and specific stress points on the journey. For example:

- The Executive Team makes final decisions, commits strategic resources and budget.

- Business Unit Leaders provide day-to-day guidance and leadership for the project team.

- Managers prepare new marketing processes and prepare their teams.

- Functional leaders provide much needed support from IT, HR and Finance.

- Marketers train and prepare to use new marketing processes and technologies.

- A Project Team designs the new processes, develops offers and campaigns, designs and produces new creative assets, configures new enabling marketing technologies, executes the strategy in the market and measures the impact.

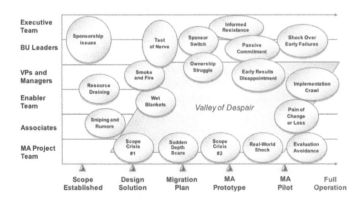

Transformational Marketing Stakeholder Stress Points

Here's some good news: the stress points for each stakeholder are predictable and can be managed to ensure success. By the way, our goal here is not to avoid the stress involved with a high-speed thrill ride, you're going to get that no matter what! Our goal is to point out what creates the anxiety and give you some ways to help different people on your team deal with it proactively.

To help you understand and identify the stress points on your own team, here are several examples across a marketing program timeline including quotes from different stakeholders:

Stress Points as Marketing Transformation Scope is Being Established

- Sponsorship Issues: "Obviously, this is going to need close coordination with ongoing campaigns. This can be an aggressive addition to our Customer Retention program."

- Resource Draining: "Look, I know John is an important member of your Marketing team, but I need him back. I just lost Jane."

- Sniping and Rumors: "They say this is all about automating some of the heavy lifting that we do today in running campaigns, but it doesn't take a genius to figure out that this is going to result in layoffs on the marketing team."

- Scope Crisis #1: "To get to the bottom-line benefits we're after, we need to immediately evaluate all of our existing customer touchpoints with a new marketing automation system."

Stress Points as Transformational Marketing Project is Created and Execution Plan is Proposed

- Test of Nerve: "You've shown us the customer personas, the journey map and a marketing playbook based on a bunch of assumptions and things that we just don't know yet -- and how much money do you want for the first phase?"

- Smoke and Fire: "I really don't understand why we are focusing on building a new customer acquisition campaign -- we all know that inbound marketing is not consistent with our feet-on-the-street sales strategy."

- Wet Blankets: "The new Marketing workflow looks fine, but you are asking us to integrate customer data from more source systems in six months than we've done in six years."

- Sudden Depth Scare: "Wow, if we've got to write out the business rules for every major exception to this Marketing process, we'll be sitting here writing them until next year. They're out of their minds."

Stress Points as Marketing Transformation Moves into the Prototype Phase

- Sponsor Switch: "I'm absolutely overwhelmed. I can't even begin to spend enough time with the Marketing team -- I need to dish responsibility for the project to John."

- Ownership Struggle: "Look, I'm responsible for the bottom line around here, so I'm going to call the shots."

- Scope Crisis #2: "Okay, if we try to do everything in this Marketing plan, we'll need 26 creative teams, 7 pilot processes and over 50% of the company working on this half-time."

Stress Points as Transformational Marketing Moves into the Pilot Phase

- Informed Resistance: "This is not the way to run a high-performance marketing team and it's certainly not the way we got here."

- Passive Commitment: "The inbound marketing strategy and marketing automation tools look very promising but I'm going to wait and see how things develop before I commit more attention to this effort for my business."

- Early Results Disappointment: "We were supposed to increase the quality and the number of Sales Qualified Leads by 5x. After six weeks, we're actually seeing fewer leads, lower productivity and our best sales guys are grumbling."

- Real-World Shock: "I can't believe they're still not entering correct data about customer interactions and continuing to waste our time -- these guys just don't get what we're trying to do with this initiative!"

Stress Points as Transformational Marketing Moves into Full Operation and Organizational Adoption

- Shock over Early Failures: "It's working for that business unit. I want to know why it isn't working for all of them!"

- Implementation Crawl: "I think we need to take more time to understand this breakdown in that business until before we go any further."

- Pain of Change or Loss: "I took this job because I liked being able to do my own thing— coming to work is never going to be the same again."

- Evaluation Avoidance: "We better let this new lead nurturing campaign run a few more months before we can be clear on how well it works."

By understanding and identifying the stakeholder stress points up front, your eyes are now fully open and you're looking forward. You can't completely avoid the stress points. Some level of tension and anxiety may actually help you achieve our goals with transformational marketing.

So, what do we need to get in place before we strap in and leave the station on our journey? How can we navigate the stress points, avoid the pitfalls and generate the creative tension that will help catapult us to the next level of marketing performance?

How do we ensure that the conditions for success remain in place throughout the project and stress and tension do not overwhelm the project team?

Conducting a Transformational Marketing Conditions for Success Diagnostic

Our research has revealed five conditions for success in marketing initiatives involving significant change. We have developed a diagnostic framework that can be used with project teams during the initial scoping of the transformational marketing journey and routinely in subsequent phase of the implementation effort. Below are abbreviated definitions from the diagnostic and some illustrations of the success markers for each area.

Explicit Value

There must be a mutually agreed business outcome that is clearly defined and measurable in terms of strategic, operational, economic and organizational benefit; and a case for user adoption at the individual level.

If the following is true, you will know that your transformational marketing program is tied to explicit value:

- There is a shared understanding of the desired business outcome.

- There is a business case for justifying the investment and quantifying the expected return.

- There is a clear definition of what success looks like.

- There are measures and metrics established to track the impact of the initiative across key performance dimensions:

  - Strategic

  - Operational

  - Economic

  - Organizational

- Employees see the reasons for change and are active adopters.

Full Alignment

Key executives and stakeholders are fully aligned on the priority of the effort and achievement of intended outcomes. Informed understanding and intention among all the key stakeholders regarding the complete transformational journey to results, including visibility to potential challenges and operational implications.

You will know your team is fully aligned if:

- Decisions don't get revisited over and over.

- Discussions are well structured—not a chaotic mix of clarifying problem, proposing solutions and discussing implications.

- People feel that they are being heard and understood.

- Decisions do not divide the group into winners and losers.

- Decisions are made with an understanding of implications.

- It's clear how to decide (vote, consensus, mandate).

- Once a decision is made, next steps are crystal clear.

- Decisions being implemented are not frequently reconsidered.

- People support the decision once it is made.

Sponsorship and Accountability

An executive leader or executive leadership team is in place with the positional authority, credibility, skill, resolve, and time to get the transformational marketing program moving, and maintain its momentum through to results. Importantly, leadership is personally "at stake" in the journey.

You will know you have sufficient sponsorship and accountability if:

- The executive sponsor has a track record of leading the organization through a change effort in the past.

- Sponsor has a scope of authority, power or influence commensurate with the scope of change involved.

- Team leaders have strong relationship with key stakeholders.

- Leaders appear to the team as "in the game" and are held personally accountable for their action/inaction.

- Leaders are highly credible and command organizational respect

- Leaders have demonstrated an ability to:

  - Make decisions

  - Influence others

  - Admit doubt or failure

  - Accept criticism

  - Deliver criticism effectively

  - Make things happen

Organizational Commitment

It is imperative to root out "passive" commitment to the project and/or passive aggressive behaviors. Marketing leaders must take personal responsibility for the program, are fighting for success and take sides on conflicts and difficult issues.

You will know that you are dealing with PASSIVE commitment if:

- Resources on the program are the best people *available.*

- A steering committee just *monitors progress and manages costs.*

- Communication to the workforce occurs *only* when requested by the program manager.

- Responsibility for managing conflicts *is delegated* to the project manager.

- Leaders *maintain a "proper" distance* from the initiative to ensure that its needs are balanced against the demands of other projects.

By contrast, you will know you are generating ACTIVE commitment if:

- Resources on the program are people who are **really important** to the business.

- The steering committee **surfaces conflicts and manages risks.**

- There are communications on the importance of transforming marketing for the business at **every available opportunity.**

- Leaders are taking **personal responsibility** for managing any major conflicts raised.

- Executives are publicly and passionately declaring sponsorship and support for the transformational marketing program—and they are **seen to take sides**!

Performance Management

Scope for the program must be appropriate to obtain the business results desired; neither so broad nor so narrow as to jeopardize success. A performance evaluation process is in place to ensure that the program is appropriately staffed with high-quality, high performing talent who represent the cross-functional expertise needed for success. Rapid, agile implementation plan is in place and agreed to by all involved parties.

You will know that scope, team and time are in balance if you are proactively managing the undercurrents of a transformational marketing program.

- Expectations
  - Clear demands on project teams
  - Clear understanding of needed business results and timing
  - Scope aligned with desired results
  - Communication of purpose, timing and process of change
  - Clear boundaries for change are set
  - Clear link to personal/individual expectations
- Energy
  - Balancing of work/play
  - Learning by doing
  - Celebrating key milestones
  - Nurturing involvement
  - Practicing "straight talk" and honesty
  - No "painfully polite" conversations
  - Rewarding and recognizing value creation clearly
- Myths
  - Modeling of new/desired behaviors
  - Sharing of new success stories
  - No reminiscing on better times

- Confronting sacred cows

- Open discussions of what ought to be

- Obsolete notions of marketing are rejected

Generating Creative Tension for Transformational Marketing Success

The stress of transformational change is accompanied by a sharp decline in performance at the individual and team level. We refer to this phenomenon of declining performance as the **"Valley of Despair"**, which is characterized by a steep fall in productivity, followed by a slow rise to previously established performance levels.

As the organization emerges from the "Valley" and overall marketing productivity rapidly increases, a new form of stress and tension will occur. During this part of the journey, your people will begin speculating that there is another steep decline just over the next rise. The reality is that there is a gap between the promise of where you are headed and the reality of where you are. This results in additional organization tension, but in this case, it can also be **a source of new energy for the team working on the transformational marketing initiative.**

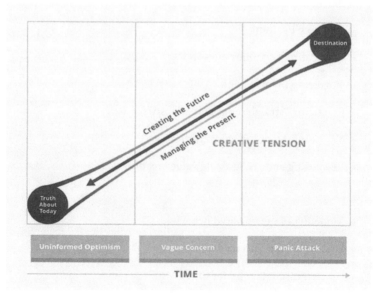

"The gap between vision and current reality is also a source of energy. If there were no gap, there would be no need for any action to move towards the vision."

— Peter Senge, The Fifth Discipline

Under the right circumstances, as pointed out by Peter Senge, this kind of tension can help facilitate creativity and increase your team's ability to change. Generating this kind of **creative tension** requires clarity about your desired brand destination and full organizational alignment on the "truth about today." In other words, the gap and desired outcome need to be clear so people are motivated to change. When properly directed and harnessed, a little organizational tension is not necessarily a bad thing.

Creative tension is a behavioral adaptation that magnifies creativity and facilitates transformational change.

When you clearly articulate your brand destination and the gap between your destination and your current reality, you create emotional and energetic tension that seeks to be resolved. Robert Fritz, the author best known for his work on "structural dynamics", calls this a ***tension-resolution system***. Fritz helps us visualize by using the metaphor of stretching a rubber band—as you stretch it, this creates tension, and the tendency of the rubber band is to pull back to resolve the tension in the system.

Imagine that your destination is represented by your right hand and your current reality is represented by your left hand, with the rubber band around both hands. The greater the gap between your destination and your reality, the more the rubber band will stretch, the greater the tension, and the stronger the motivation and energy will be to resolve that tension. And hopefully, the rubber band does not snap!

Your team will be highly motivated to alleviate cognitive dissonance by closing the gap between your current reality and your destination. This allows you to release more energy, resources, and creativity into finding ways to close that gap.

It turns out that this can be a very productive and good form of stress or "eustress." As marketers, when **we are faced with an unresolved issue or a big**

challenge, this triggers us to perform at our peak and release more energy into dealing with the problem, and generating solutions for better results.

Betty Edwards, in her book, *Drawing on the Right Side of the Brain*, talks about how we usually tackle problems with our left-brain-directed thinking first. If the left-brain can't solve the problem, it automatically shifts the problem over to the right-brain. When we have creative tension, the left-brain is more willing to shift the problem over for the right-brain. That's when you start to find more creative solutions.

Clearly, there are lots of different names for creative tension and lots of different models for generating it for good purpose. Creative tension is based on an understanding of how our minds control the management of our attention, energy, and creativity. It's critical to use that understanding to build a structure that creates an energy that seeks to be resolved — what Robert Fritz calls the "path of least resistance" — and to flick the switch so that we can apply our best thinking to the issue. If you want to successfully leverage creative tension for your Transformational marketing team, focus on three things:

1. **Clearly articulate your brand destination in as much detail as you can.** Don't worry about using metrics and goals. Just ask yourself the question, "What does success look like?" It's also important that you're describing a destination, and not an anti-destination. A destination talks about what you want, while an anti-destination is focused on what you don't want. Focusing on what you don't want makes your mind associate back into current and past problems, so it serves to reinforce the problem, instead of generating the desired creative tension.

2. **Tell the truth about today.** If you're pretending that you're somewhere you're not, you'll reduce the creative tension and run the risk of choosing irrelevant strategies to get to your desired destination. Watch, listen, and pay attention to the present. Ask for feedback and opinions from other people to get varying perspectives on your current reality. Question all your stories about reality so that you can peel away the self-deception and get to the core truth of what your current reality is all about.

3. **Build "how" bridges.** Pay attention to defining the next obvious steps for bridging your current reality to your destination. You won't necessarily know the full "how to get there" at the outset, but as you keep refining and articulating your perception of reality and your destination and keep taking the next obvious steps, you can trust that the creative tension will seek to resolve itself by getting you to where you want to be.

Sometimes creative tension can feel pretty nasty—especially if you're not well practiced in using it. It feels a lot like mental anxiety and it's easy to get wound up with so much stress that you can't think clearly and it all just feels bad. One of the tricky things about creative tension is that there's a sweet spot where the anxiety levels are "just right" to release your peak performance and best thinking. Too much stress and anxiety and you'll drop into *distress*, and your performance and the quality of your thinking will plummet with it. So, don't go pushing yourself to articulate a ridiculously huge destination in the hope that creative tension will get you there. Big, hairy audacious goals for your transformational marketing implementation are not always appropriate. **It's key to set up realistic goals!**

Here are some suggestions from Cath Duncan at Agile Living that we believe will help you prevent creative tension from becoming unproductive stress for your transformational marketing program team:

By understanding and identifying the ways to generate creative tension, you now have a great opportunity to magnify organizational creativity and facilitate the transformational changes you need for a successful journey.

Transformational marketing is about optimizing and mobilizing all marketing assets to create lasting preference for the brand, to activate customer purchase intent, and to accelerate organic growth of revenues and profits. To truly transform marketing and put powerful marketing systems in place to execute with ruthless consistency, you need to ensure that the conditions for success are in place before you start out on your journey. Periodically, you need to check in with the team; run the diagnostic; generate and focus creative tension; and assure that you don't get lost along the way.

7 TIPS to AVOID UNPRODUCTIVE STRESS

1 Maintain a playful attitude. You can be clear on what you're aiming for, but don't take yourself too seriously. Try to see obstacles and failures as being all part of the game, making the game more interesting.

2 Avoid dwelling on mistakes or failures—negative self-talk can quickly tip you over from eustress into distress, where your performance and the quality of your thinking drop.

3 Notice when you're resisting reality and practice letting go of the need to force things to go your way.

4 Stay open to different ways that you could close the gap between reality and your destination. Hold fast to your "what" — your brand destination of what you want to create — but be very loose about your "how" — how you create it.

5 Don't entertain anxiety from other people who are struggling with the gap. Their anxiety about the presence of that gap can make you overly anxious about it, which can tip you from eustress into stress.

6 Hang out with people who can tolerate creative tension and who won't try to talk you into changing your destination just so they can feel more comfortable about your choices.

7 Resist complaining about not being where you want to be — to yourself or to other people. This increases frustration and can make the creative tension unbearable.

Chapter 19

Driving Innovation Through Marketing Systems

Big box toy retailer, Toys "R" Us, has filed for Chapter 11 bankruptcy protection and is officially lost in transformation. The company pointed to a looming deadline to pay back $400 million of the $5 billion in long-term debt on their balance sheet for why they filed in advance of their all-important holiday season. The timing couldn't be worse. The toy business is incredibly seasonal, more than 40% of the company's sales come in during the fourth quarter of the year. Even though the company announced that it is not immediately closing any of its 1,600 stores, the bankruptcy filing signals instability to skittish toy suppliers and certainly puts shoppers "in play" to consider Wal-Mart, Target and Amazon for their holiday purchases.

"A lot of people hear the word bankruptcy and they immediately conclude
that the brand or the company is going to go away"
— Dave Brandon, CEO Toys "R" Us

Bankruptcy experts assert that Toys "R" Us is just running into the same head-winds that forced other big box retailers to file for Chapter 11: too much under-utilized real estate. While excessive debt and real estate overhang are contributing to the demise of the company, quite frankly, their real problem is far more severe. Here are the three key reasons why Toys "R" Us is going bankrupt and why their proposed turnaround actions may be futile:

Their brand story has lost its relevance. Toys "R" Us is failing because the brand story is no longer relevant—not because people have stopped buying toys. According to the National Retail Federation, U.S. holiday sales grew 4 percent to $658.3 billion last year and they are forecast to grow 6 percent more this coming year. The fact is, people are still buying toys, they're just not buying them at Toys "R" Us.

"We all know retail is not dead or dying, but it's certainly transforming."
— Matthew Shay, CEO, National Retail Foundation

With more than 65 years in the toy business, the Toys"R"Us brand story has always centered on being the "toy authority" for parents and children alike. Do you remember Beanie Babies, Tickle Me Elmo, Furbies and Pokémon—the most sought-after holiday toys? The toys that your mom was willing to wrestle out of the hands of a complete stranger in the store?

Let's face it: Toys "R" Us was *the place* to get the hottest new toys and they had knowledgeable sales staff who would point you in the right direction during the holiday season. The brand story was about quality, value, selection and an in-store shopping experience focused on *making the shopper the "hero."*

Today, however, no one *wants* to be in a Toys "R" Us store during the holi-days—not even the desperate last-minute shoppers! Of course, shoppers still want to be the hero and score that hot new toy, but they don't want to wait in long lines and risk getting into a fistfight with a distraught parent in the process.

With detailed online reviews to inform purchase decisions and same day delivery service from Amazon, dad was a superhero last year when that Minecraft Lego Kit showed up at the front door the day before Christmas!

Their strategy is still misaligned. Back in early 2014, Toys "R" Us announced its "TRU Transformation" strategy to address shopper experience challenges and position the company for growth. The broad strategy included inventory management improvements, decluttering of stores, a clearer pricing strategy and simpler promotional offers for shoppers. The company also promised to integrate its in-store and online businesses more fully. And this is where they have failed.

"Those endless aisles pale in comparison with what's available online, and rock-bottom prices can be found at Amazon, Walmart, and Target."

— Greg Satell, DigitalTonto

Most people today are "hybrid" shoppers—using both online and physical retail locations as part of their buying journey. For example, they may do their browsing and research online and then make a "targeted strike" to a bricks and mortar store to buy the toy they want. Although shoppers won't ever ditch physical stores entirely, they are shifting most of their holiday toy shopping online because cluttered stores and slow-moving checkout lines deter them. Moreover, Amazon has conditioned shoppers to expect instant gratification. To make that happen, e-retailers have shifted from having a few massive, centralized distribution centers to many smaller, quick-response hubs close to large population centers. Toys "R" Us is still stuck with these massive centers which makes it difficult for them to truly integrate their online and offline businesses and respond with the speed and nimbleness that shoppers demand.

Their recent moves to upgrade systems are too little and too late. While Toys "R" Us has been minding the store, it admits that it fell behind on its e-commerce systems. Now the company is making some big bets to try to close the gaps in their systems. Their revamp is part of a nearly $100 million investment over the last three years that is geared toward jump-starting an online experience that it acknowledges lagged some of its retail peers.

"In a year to two years, we have to catch up on 10 years of innovation and that's no small feat."

— Lance Wills, Global Chief Technology Officer, Toys "R" Us

They also recently announced that they will be offering a new augmented reality (AR) in-store experience for parents and their children. Geoffrey the Giraffe, the iconic Toys "R" Us mascot, will greet shoppers on their smartphone when they enter a store. Guided by flashing icons in the aisles, shoppers will point their mobile devices at toys on shelves activating a personalized experience on their screen. For instance, in the Barbie section of the store, a virtual version of a doll on the shelf comes to life, tells her story and engages with the young shopper. Will kids convince their parents to take them into their local Toy "R" Us so they can have fun and experience AR? Absolutely. And then, the parents will still go online to buy toys for the holidays. Quite frankly, AR seems more like a win for the manufacturer rather than the retailer in this case. Janie is still going to get her Barbie… but Amazon is going to get the sale!

Frankly, it seems like the folks at Toys "R" Us are just trying to distract us with bright shiny objects. Systems have become their Story—rather than Systems enabling an authentic and relevant Story. That's not innovation, it's just a ruse to get through another holiday season. Yes, AR has the potential to deliver a remarkable shopper experience in-store, but for Toys "R" Us, it's like putting a band aid on a clogged artery and expecting it to heal.

Rest peacefully Toys "R" Us and take comfort in knowing you're not alone. You're on a well-worn path that's included many former retail category killers like Blockbuster, Circuit City, Payless Shoe Source and Sports Authority. **Turnarounds at this scale require a compelling *Story* where the shopper is the hero, a *Strategy* delivering a remarkable shopper experience and *Systems* executed with ruthless consistency.** Chasing bright shiny objects like AR and attempting to lure customers back with interruptive online campaigns and in-store communications is not innovative.

By contrast, consider the story of Chick-fil-A. Chick-fil-A introduced the famous "Eat Mor Chikin" tagline on a billboard in 1995. At the time, the company was facing stiff competition in a crowded market dominated by deep-pocketed, entrenched players like McDonald's and Burger King. Leadership at the company knew that they would it would take something special to break through to customers. They landed on a crazy, yet totally inspired idea. If you want to sell more chicken who or what has a vested interest in getting people to eat more chicken? Well, cows of course! This simple and clear story helped Chick-fil-A become the top chicken chain in the United States, the country's 8th-largest U.S. restaurant chain with more than $6 billion in annual sales.

Yet, like all transformative marketers, the team at Chick-fil-A doesn't rest on their laurels. They know that to continue to build their business they must find ways to delight customers and deepen relationships every day. That's why the company periodically makes strategic moves to boost its Brand Story, revisit their Strategy, and assure that the right Systems are aligned to execute with ruthless consistency.

After more than 22 years working with The Richards Group, Chick-fil-A ended its relationship with the agency, shaking things up for the brand. The now famous cows, created by advertising legend Stan Richards, were enshrined in the Advertising Hall of Fame and earned their place in the Smithsonian Museum in July 2015.

"No Mor Kows?"

Does the change to a new agency signal a move away from the wildly successful "spokes-cows"? Hardly. They're not completely crazy!

The leadership team at Chick-fil-A now refers to their marketing strategy as "Kows-plus", building on their tremendous brand equity. But perhaps, they are tipping their hand that they will be relying a bit less on their iconic mascots in the future. Their strategic goal is to amplify the brand's message by emotionally connecting and building relationships with new and existing customers through new stories.

"While the cows will remain an essential part of our brand, we are also working on new stories to tell. To do that, we are moving to a new strategic model to enable innovation and brand growth nationwide."

— Jon Bridges, Chief Marketing Officer at Chick-fil-A

Boosting (not Blurring) the Brand Story

Chick-fil-A's new "Kows-plus" initiative is designed to move the brand story beyond the cows. The idea is to tell a compelling story focusing on the chain's competitive advantage, and highlight topics such as quality of food, customer service, and offerings that may not have fit well into the cow theme.

"The cows are an integral part of the brand. They're our mascot if you will. But they aren't the brand. The brand is bigger than that."

— Jon Bridges, Chief Marketing Officer at Chick-fil-A

Branding is all about storytelling—the story of your brand—the advertising images and copy may be part of it, but the heart of the brand story is *why* you do what you do, and why that matters to your customers. Chick-fil-A is innovating around the existing narrative and raising the bar to focus on creating a comprehensive and compelling brand story of why Chick-fil-A does what it does, with the goal to deliver more value to its customers.

Refining the Strategy to Create More Raving Fans

The new "Kows-plus" strategy will enable the brand to focus on its core competencies and differentiate its best-in-class products and services.

> *"Ask yourself how you can deliver more value to your customers, not get more money from them."*
> — David Salyers, VP of Brand Activation at Chick-fil-A

Delivering a productive and profitable customer experience is at the heart of the Chick-fil-A strategy. Chick-fil-A aspires to create "Raving Fans," customers who are happy to pay full price, come to the store more often and tell other people about Chick-fil-A. For customers, value equals what they get divided by what they pay, so the goal is to charge the right price and focus on the numerator (what they get) to actually create value for the brand's customers.

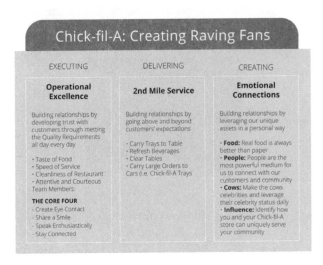

Chick-fil-A looks for ways to create valuable customer experiences by delivering quality through its products and services. The "Kows-plus" approach is a path to shift the brand's focus on creating more personalized customer experiences through the chain's key competitive advantages. If you ask a Chick-fil-A Raving Fan to share their opinion, they will likely say that the food and service are so extraordinary that they don't even think of it as fast food.

Innovating Through Systems Aligned to Execute "Kows-plus"

Whether in a store, on a billboard, on the web or on a mobile device, Chick-fil-A people don't think of customer interactions as a simple transaction; the people strive to create remarkable customer experiences. Or, as Seth Godin would say, "Experiences worthy of remark." The processes, people, and enabling platforms required at every touchpoint on the Customer BuyWay must be fully aligned to successfully bring the brand to life.

In order to accomplish this, the fast food chain strives to bring out the best in its people at every level of the organization and instill in them the values of the brand. They encourage and recognize those employees who build relationships with customers by going above and beyond customer expectations.

In the company culture, this is referred to as "second mile service. By executing with operational excellence and delivering "second mile" service, Chick-fil-A knows they can create an emotional bond with their customer that will not only differentiate the brand, but also generate advocacy. Raving fans make the Chick-fil-A story a part of their own story.

Chick-fil-A One, the restaurant's new mobile ordering app is a great example of using Systems to drive innovation.

Chick-fil-A was certainly not the first to market in the quick-serve restaurant (QSR) category with a mobile app. But by all accounts, they have one of the best in the industry because the app was specifically designed to support their unique strategy and story. The mobile app eliminates the painful experience of waiting in a long line, giving the customer the chance to place their order from their phone. To launch the mobile ordering service, the brand offered a free Chick-fil-A sandwich to anyone who downloaded the app and created an account.

On the campaign launch date, the app went from receiving an average of about 1,500 downloads daily to approximately 400,000 downloads per day. Consider for a moment the data comparing Chick-fil-A One adoption to the mobile apps to fellow QSR competitors who barely have a pulse! It turns out that a free Chick-fil-A sandwich is a pretty good driver of online behavior!

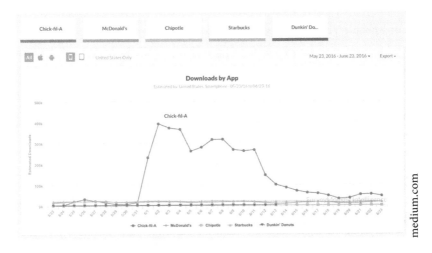

"Treat your company culture like the ultimate competitive advantage"
— David Salyers, VP of Brand Activation at Chick-fil-A

The app also enables the customer to earn free food based on a running history of their purchases. Rewards are referred to as "Treats," and the app features a graphical representation of how close you are to earning your next "Treat" like waffle fries, soft-serve ice cream, or a fruit cup (yeah right!).

Truly characteristic of the "second mile service" brand promise, the app allows you to personalize your order in ways you probably never even thought of. Add bacon to that grilled chicken sandwich? Sure, everything is better with bacon! No ice in your sweet tea? No problem. No pickles on that fried chicken sandwich? Turn your nose up to a Southern tradition? Whatever.

"Kows in Vertual Realitee"?

Of course, the spokes-cows, with their provocative and humorous personalities, continue to play a starring role in Chick-fil-A's brand story as a fun way to connect and engage with customers. Turns out, they will also be playing an important role as ambassadors (ambassa-cows?) for Chick-fil-A's experimentation with innovative technologies.

The cows are currently focused on leading the way for the brand in experimentation with virtual reality. And they want to want to share their discoveries with the world. In new Chick-fil-A brand stories, the cows are seen gifting unsuspecting people Virtual Reality (VR) headsets.

While virtual reality is new for Chick-fil-A and the Kows, it has been a winning formula for their new agency, McCann. The agency's collaboration with Framestore on Lockheed Martin's "Field Trip to Mars" campaign won 19 Cannes Lions, making it the most-awarded advertising campaign at Cannes in 2016. The virtual reality experience was designed to show school children what Mars looks like.

The Kows may be jumping into VR at just the right time. The VR consumer adoption trend line shows no signs of downturn. Samsung recently announced it has sold 5 million Gear VR headsets, and a new report from Super Data estimates 6.3 million VR headsets were shipped in 2016. By 2020, Forrester predicts that there will be 52 million units of VR headsets, or goggles, in circulation.

VR may hold the key to helping marketers break through the clutter and open doors to unimaginable storytelling possibilities. Why? Because VR allows building brand awareness, while authentically engaging consumers in productive ways:

- It's completely immersive—users wearing a VR headset are completely immersed in the content, which means fewer distractions and more attention on the brand story;

- It delivers high impact—the intensity of a VR experience is greater than traditional media generating strong emotions for its users which are linked to real behavior change;

- It generates lasting memories—our brains are built to remember events linked to locations, this means that VR experiences have a longer trace in the audience's memory;

- It's cool and novel—with high media and public interest in VR, early adopters will continue to benefit from favorable media exposure.

Today, Chick-fil-A generates more revenue per restaurant than any other fast-food chain. They have shown patience and diligence in how they put Systems in place that help them execute with operational excellence while not distracting from or blurring their brand story. The brand understands the importance of finding new, innovative ways to tell their brand story and create delightful customer experiences that make people want to engage, want to learn more, and want to advocate for Chick-fil-A. So, are you ready to "Stik ur fase in vertual realitee and git ur hooman mindz blown?"

Chapter 20

Unleashing the Ghost in the Machine

www.flickr.com/photos/
peterhellberg/2308864066/

Meet Evisu, a premium denim and lifestyle brand with a global presence. Like all global brands, their goal is to engage their customers with the right message, at the right time, through the right channel and with content that's relevant and timely.

They have a very small online team, and managing all their digital marketing needs, specifically, SEM and Social channels, is an overwhelming task. The brand turned to Albert, the first artificial intelligence marketing platform for the enterprise. Albert removes the complexities of modern marketing by performing many of the time-consuming, manual tasks which humans are unable to perform at the speed and scale required for efficient and effective consumer interactions.

Before using Albert, Evisu was running campaigns on a global scale, with a distinct lack of specific geo-targeting. Albert was able to pinpoint which countries and specific cities they could get the most engagement and allowed them to redirect their efforts to targeted regions. More importantly, Albert discovered never-before-known high-value audiences. For example, Albert determined that Facebook users with the occupation "Engineer" engaged 300 percent more with Evisu's ads than other Facebook users. This led to a significant boost in conversions on social campaigns, where they had previously had little success.

Stop Thinking Campaigns and Start Thinking Conversations

The multitude of mediums and technologies that are being used to speak to the marketplace is revolutionizing how the work of marketing is performed. The days of *campaigns*—the practice of start-stop-measure-tweak-repeat—are over. Today, for marketing to build brands and drive revenue, it must facilitate a continuous, meaningful *conversation* with customers.

Traditional marketing campaigns are sponsored by the brand owner and are demarcated by periodic sales seasons, budget cycles, product launches or responses to disruptive market forces. A campaign may last a day or a month, but if we're thinking about it as having a fixed start, middle and end, we may miss the opportunity to focus on the bigger picture—the idea that a winning marketing strategy must be adaptive and integrated across channels.

By initiating and engaging in conversations, Marketing can take advantage of the immediacy and the reach that technology has provided us with social media and email to communicate with our audience continuously and meaningfully, targeting our message by media type and inviting the recipients of that message to engage with us and respond.

These traditional outbound marketing campaigns are far less effective at winning and retaining customers than they once were. To achieve sustainable growth in today's always-connected, real-time world, marketers must deliver continuous, customized, two-way, insight-driven interactions with customers on an individual level.

Brands that understand this and put the right Systems in place to scale are creating competitive advantages that are very difficult for their competitors to replicate because it's not just about technology. It's about delivering the perfect combination of content and context: the right Story, the right Strategy, and the right Systems. Forrester Research refers to this as creating a "Contextual Marketing Engine."

In their 2016 survey of 115 technology, marketing, and customer experience professionals, Forrester found that, across the board, organizations' investments revolve around implementing customer personalization initiatives, solving people's challenges, and assembling digital experience systems.

Forrester analysts suggest that contextual marketing engines create sticky, highly engaging environments for customer interactions. These Systems also yield proprietary data that you cannot replicate with traditional marketing methods or purchase from third-party data sources. The results translate into unprecedented levels of customer engagement, increased revenue, and better product experiences.

One company that is leading the way is Nike. In the three years leading up to 2012, Nike decreased their advertising spend in mass media channels in the US by 40 percent and still managed to grow the company by $9 billion in three years. They deliberately pulled back on their traditional outbound campaign spending.

So, what was the secret to Nike's growth strategy? The answer: contextual marketing.

Nike began using customer health data collected from devices such as the FuelBand to nudge consumers back to its digital platform NikePlus every day. NikePlus is a contextual marketing engine that uses social sharing and fitness contests to generate more interactions, creating a scale that rivals paid media. At the end of the first year of operation, Nike Plus had 18 million members, with 15,000 joining each day.

The truth is that most of us don't have the resources and/or the brand equity of a Nike to pull off this kind of transformation. For most marketers, we struggle mightily to practice contextual marketing at scale. That is, managing real-time coordination of digital interactions across all channels, with the right customer and the right message, at the right moment… It may be easy to say, but it's hard to execute. Why?

Here are several reasons why contextual marketing is such an onerous task for marketers and why Artificial Intelligence will transform the discipline of marketing in the immediate future.

5 REASONS WHY ARTIFICIAL INTELLIGENCE
WILL TRANSFORM MARKETING AS WE KNOW IT

1 Big Data Begets Big Complexity

Machines are much better equipped to unravel the enormous complexities born from big data.

2 Technology Amplifies the Gap Between Strategy & Systems

As newer and more sophisticated technologies become available, the gap between a marketer's time spent on Strategy versus Systems will continue to widen and leaders will seek alternative approaches to close that gap.

3 Demand for Customized Conversations & Personalized Experiences Accelerates

Marketers can't deliver personalized experiences without having the right Systems in place. They need to understand the customer and take immediate action to engage them at the 'moment of truth.'

4 Data May Be Valuable as the Brand Itself

With AI, there is no reason why a brand couldn't manage the execution in house, own the data, glean insights dynamically, optimize offer efficiency and grow revenues.

5 Marketing & Innovation Produce Results

CMOs will seek out innovative AI-based Systems to execute their Strategies to deliver revenue growth and cost reductions — while mitigating the risk of damaging customer relationships and ultimately tarnishing the brand.

1. **Big Data Begets Big Complexity**. Let's face it: there are so many channels, devices, and segments creating so much data that it's nearly impossible to do personalization and contextual marketing at scale. Humans are just not capable of wrapping their heads around the data, and they can't possibly test the thousands, and perhaps millions, of messaging permutations to calculate the right solution for optimizing business results. Even the most talented marketers and data scientists are ultimately constrained by how much data they can identify and process. Machines are much better equipped to unravel the enormous complexities born from big data gathered continuously in an always-on, always-connected, real-time world.

2. **Technology Amplifies the Gap Between Strategy and Systems**. Most marketers are not trained to be technologists. In school, they learn about Marketing Strategy—how to research markets, segment and define them; how to understand customers and communicate with them; how to drive demand and desire, and how to communicate efficiently and effectively. It should come as no surprise that this is the kind of work that many marketers want to do.

   By contrast, rarely do marketers learn how to operate email or social media marketing platforms as part of their marketing degree program—even though this is one of the more common responsibilities for entry-level marketers. Technology vendors play an important role in providing certification programs and training, but for most marketers, much of their MarTech training is on the job.

   Thus, many businesses never know if they have the right talent to operate increasingly sophisticated marketing technologies. And, even for the most tech-savvy marketers, dealing with the integration of multiple data sources, workflows, rules engines, reporting, and analytics is a heavy lift. Often these tasks occupy so much of a marketer's time that they have far less time to spend on more strategic marketing activities.

   As newer and more sophisticated technologies become available, the gap between a marketer's time spent on Strategy versus Systems will continue to widen and leaders will seek alternative approaches to close that gap.

3. **Demand for Customized Conversations and Personalized Experiences Accelerates**. Thanks to advances by companies like Amazon, customers have come to expect more customized and personalized brand experiences. Most brands don't have the deep pockets to make the kind of Systems investments that Amazon has made over the past decade. That said, once customers get a taste of an experience they like, they hold many other brands to the same standard.

Marketers can't deliver these types of personalized experiences without having the right Systems in place. They need to understand the customer and take immediate action to engage them at the "moment of truth." That's pretty tough to do if you've outsourced your marketing (and much of your data) to agencies, or if you're counting on humans to keep up with the dynamic demands of customers and volumes of interaction data. There needs to be a better way.

4. **Data May Be as Valuable as the Brand Itself**. Customer data and insights into their relationship with a brand may end up being more valuable than the brand itself. Data has become the fuel for contextual marketing engines. Without data, there is no actionable insight. And without insight, marketers are flying blind. So, this raises an interesting question: how can a brand fully own their data if they are outsourcing execution and analysis to an agency or another third-party firm? Moreover, with the recent discovery of under-the-table rebates and lack of transparency in media buying practices, serious trust issues are raising questions about the risk and the value of outsourcing.

Artificial Intelligence platforms offer a way for marketers to bring execution, analytics, and data in-house. Agencies will certainly continue to be a great resource for ideation and creative production. However, with AI, there is no reason why a brand couldn't manage the execution in-house, own the data, glean insights dynamically, optimize offer efficiency, and grow revenues.

5. **Marketing and Innovation Produce Results; All the Rest Are Costs.** As Peter Drucker rightly pointed out: "Marketing is the distinguishing,

unique function of the business." Chief Marketing Officers have tremendous revenue growth responsibilities to the business—many CEOs are relying on their CMOs to deliver growth and ROMI (return on marketing investment).

CMOs, in general, have one of the shortest tenures in the C-suite because of the pressure and urgency to generate results. Disruptive new marketing technologies represent a double-edged sword for marketing leaders. On one hand, they offer ways to help marketers cut through the clutter, distinguish the brand, and win customers.

On the other hand, marketing technologies can just as easily cut into and damage profitable customer relationships with interruptive and irrelevant campaigns. CMOs will seek out innovative AI-based Systems to execute their Strategies to deliver revenue growth and cost reductions—all while mitigating the risk of damaging customer relationships and ultimately tarnishing the brand.

"Because the purpose of business is to create a customer, the business enterprise has two—and only two—basic functions: marketing and innovation. Marketing and innovation produce results; all the rest are costs. Marketing is the distinguishing, unique function of the business."
— Peter Drucker

The common thread behind all the reasons that AI will transform marketing is the pace of change and sheer magnitude of new technology that marketers must deal with on a daily basis.

The fact that many marketers aren't trained properly to use the technology intensifies the problem. Artificial Intelligence and Machine Learning are poised to solve many of the complexities that exist within Marketing Systems today—allowing marketers to get back to what they've always been good at: Strategy.

commons.wikimedia.org

Consider the story of the New York Harley Davidson dealership that saw 3000 percent growth in sales leads. That kind of growth is more commonly associated with a startup, not a legacy brand like Harley. It's a real outlier—especially when it's a legacy brand so entrenched in American culture that you could argue it is synonymous with bald eagles and freedom.

So, how did this iconic brand increase their sales leads by almost 3000 percent? Predictive analytics, powered by AI and machine learning.

Predictive analytics encompasses a variety of statistical techniques from predictive modeling, machine learning, and data mining that analyze current and historical facts to make predictions about future or otherwise unknown events.

AI Systems don't need to waste effort researching and creating customer personas. They possess the processing power to plow through massive rows of data to find real customers in the field. By determining what actual online behaviors have the highest probability of resulting in conversions, the machine can then identify potential buyers online who exhibit these behaviors and begin conversing with them automatically.

At Asaf Jacobi's Harley-Davidson dealership in New York, Jacobi transformed lead generation for the business using the same AI System used by Evisu Jeans: Albert.

With help from Albert, the dealership went from getting one qualified lead per day to 40. In the first month, 15% of those new leads were "lookalikes," meaning that the people calling the dealership to set up a visit resembled previous high-value customers and therefore were more likely to make a purchase. By the third month, the dealership's leads had increased 2930%, 50% of them lookalikes, leaving Jacobi scrambling to set up a new call center with six new employees to handle all the new business.

At Jacobi's dealership today, Albert performs many of the time-consuming, manual tasks which human marketers are unable to perform at the speed and scale required for efficient and effective customer interactions. The AI tool enhances overall marketing productivity by complementing the role of human marketers.

Man versus Machine?

Quite frankly, some people have a healthy fear of Artificial Intelligence (AI) and the potential for unintended consequences of a future where machines have taken control of the world and reign over humans (think about the plot of *The Matrix* or *The Terminator*).

Although experts predict that one-third of our jobs will be replaced by robots by 2025, this isn't a reason to worry — it just means it's time to adapt. The true losers of the AI and Machine Learning economic shift will be the laggards and late-adopters during this transition.

The transformative nature of Artificial Intelligence (AI) technologies and Machine Learning will be far reaching. Machine Learning will drive an entirely new wave of software applications and platforms that can revolutionize human-computer interaction, and much like the Internet, social media, and mobility waves, it will redefine entire consumer and enterprise markets.

Machine learning is a specific method of data analysis that automates analytical model building. Using algorithms that iteratively learn from data, machine learning allows computers to find hidden insights without being explicitly programmed where to look. Machine learning is the area of AI that will have the biggest impact on the discipline of Marketing in the next 5-10 years.

As we have seen with other disruptive technologies in different sectors of our economy, machines are better suited to perform certain types of tasks than humans. Likewise, humans are better suited to perform certain tasks than machines. And perhaps most interesting, there are process areas where humans and machines can complement each other to optimize productivity.

From marketing operations to marketing execution to customer engagement and marketing analytics, AI will transform the way that marketers work. AI will not only enhance overall marketing productivity by complementing the role of human marketers but also replace the role of humans in many parts of the marketing organization. In the chart below, we've characterized the type of tasks where machines outperform humans and vice-versa.

A Framework for Predicting the Winners and Losers

Today's marketers need to prepare for the revolution of AI and machine learning, and clearly articulate how they will utilize artificial intelligence to enhance customer experiences, increase ROI, and boost operations efficiency. We've developed a framework to help marketers begin to understand how AI, and more specifically, machine learning will disrupt the traditional "marketing value chain."

Like most processes across the various functions of a business, not all marketing processes are the same. Even within the marketing department, processes can be very different in terms of their basic characteristics. Marketing processes can be characterized by three dimensions:

Level of Complexity. Complexity is the degree of difficulty that marketers experience in collaboration, coordination, and decision-making to get their work done. An example of a low complexity process might be sending out an email. High complexity processes might include things like customer data mining, predictive modeling, strategic planning and creative design.

Level of Predictability. Predictability is the degree of difficulty for a marketer to determine in advance the way a process will be executed. Low predictability process examples might include managing customer interactions on social media channels. High predictability processes might include handling marketing budget requests.

Level of Repetitiveness. Repetitiveness is the frequency that a marketer executes the process. A process executed only once a year has a lower degree of repetitiveness than a process executed every day. Examples of a low repetitiveness process might be developing a brand architecture for a new product. A high repetitiveness process might be managing an online chat with prospective customers.

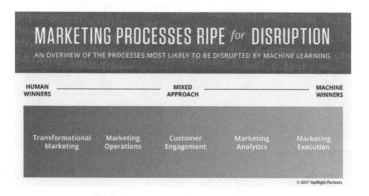

Broadly speaking, marketing processes with high complexity, high predictability, and high repetitiveness are logical targets to be managed by machines. Most Marketing Execution and Marketing Analytics processes fit this characterization and we expect that AI will likely replace most human activities in these areas over the next several years.

By contrast, marketing processes with low predictability are not seen as good targets to be managed by machines. It is challenging for a machine to design and adopt new procedures "on the fly." Low predictability processes require the marketer to exercise judgment and apply originality to define alternative solutions and/or redefine processes, thus being an area in which humans excel.

As AI continues to pervade our everyday lives, the next generation of marketers will be "AI natives," much like the prior generations of "mobile and digital natives.." They will have a redefined relationship with technology, which will further remove elements of friction in daily activities, making room for increased productivity and creativity.

"Prediction has always been critical to marketing planning and responsiveness, but this was done by marketers to anticipate what consumers would buy. In the future, consumers will be using predictive tools that will decide what to buy for them."
— J Walker Smith, Chief Knowledge Officer,
Brand and Marketing, Kantar Consulting

Are the marketing and advertising industries ready to scale AI? Not quite. But there are signs of disruption. Agencies are building services on top of AI technologies, and there are already some mature AI-based marketing technologies established that go well beyond audience targeting. These early adopters are gaining an advantage through the proper use of the new tools.

There's little doubt that AI will transform marketing as we know it. As new technology emerges, it's more important than ever for marketers to get the basics right.

According to a research report by OneSpot and Marketing Insider Group, nearly half of consumers won't spend time with branded content if it's not relevant to their interests. 88% of consumers say that personally relevant content improves how they feel about a brand. In other words, personalized content has become more of a necessity rather than just a nice touch.

When marketers are untethered from the mundane matters of the day-to-day and allowed to focus their mind on more strategic endeavors, the results can be astounding. As we witnessed in the Evisu, Nike and Harley-Davidson stories, this is the true power and benefit of unleashing the ghost in the machine.

Conclusion

D o you remember the scene in the 2002 movie *Minority Report* when Tom Cruise walks into a shopping mall and he is bombarded with "personalized" holographic images for a variety of products? Brand stories and offers popping up all over the place interrupting him and attempting (unsuccessfully) to get his attention. Is this where technological innovation will lead us in marketing? If so, we're looking forward to an inefficient and pretty creepy future! A flood of annoying imagery, irrelevant and conflicting messaging, sensory overload, ad nauseam.

Of course, this type of real-time, personalized marketing is with us already, in a much more efficient and slightly less creepy manner. For example, consider web retargeting. You visit a website and a cookie is left on your computer. That cookie triggers targeted display advertising on other web sites as you continue to browse online.

In this way, a brand can attempt to win back your attention, remind you to go back to their web site, and perhaps even convince you to make a purchase. This is still an interruptive tactic, but if the brand story is simple, authentic and relevant, a retargeting strategy can be an efficient way to nurture your target customer and give them a reason to engage with you.

That said, retargeting still doesn't address the underlying problem with digital advertising: very few people click on traditional banners. Most people have been conditioned to tune out noise as we browse the web. This phenomenon is sometimes referred to as "banner blindness." People almost never look at anything that looks like an advertisement, whether or not it's actually an ad. Website visitors just intuitively avoid display ads when browsing their favorite web site destinations.

A study conducted by Google's Doubleclick team in March 2017 found that across all ad formats and placements, the click through rate (CTR) is just 0.05%. That equates to just 5 clicks per 10,000 impressions! This fact alone should give transformative marketers pause as they consider the potential futility of driving direct response from online display or banner ads.

So, what does the future hold for marketing? How will marketing shift from interruptive technical tricks to truly transformational innovations?

Since the early 1990's, Marketing Technology (MarTech) and Advertising Technology (AdTech) have rapidly evolved and dramatically changed how we connect, communicate, and collaborate, both as individuals and as businesses. We've witnessed the convergent waves of consumer electronics, mobility, social media, cloud computing, and big data reshape how companies go to market and connect with customers in relevant, productive and profitable ways.

Equipped with information and linked through social media, customers will only continue to gain power and learn how to exercise it. As we look ahead to the year 2020, companies will need innovations to balance this shift in market power, keep up with customer demands and prepare to respond to these trends:

- "Mass Marketing" will take on an entirely new meaning as the masses will control much of the dialog (and all of the authentic advocacy) about brands and their reputations.

- Connected Customers will demand full control over the timing and process of communications and consumption, so businesses will be expected to meet customer needs as soon as they materialize via whatever channel the customer has chosen.

- Marketing campaigns, once thought of as one-way communication paths from brand to customer, will truly become two-way streets. Continuous engagement will be the norm and episodic campaigns will be in the rear-view mirror for most companies.

- Company marketing processes and the insights and intelligence embedded within them will coalesce. Not just because they overlap so much, but because the customer experiences them as parts of the same interaction.

- Static rules-based processes will just not be able to keep up with the pace of market change. Faster, smarter and more predictive marketing processes and decision-making will be required.

The future of marketing is now. And it's going to be much better than what was portrayed in Minority Report

Based on our research at TopRight, we are expecting that Marketing Automation innovation will be shaped and governed by three significant shifts:

From Brand to Reputation Management

While you may think you or someone at your organization manages your brand today, it is really the external perception of the target audience that defines your brand. Making matters worse, social media channels give your target audience (and many others) an easy way to share opinions about your brand with thousands of others in an instant. This powerful and ubiquitous communication channel has the potential to put your brand in constant peril and make your firm's reputation vulnerable to rumors and viral misinformation.

This raises an interesting question for marketers in 2020: how will you manage a brand in a world where so many of the success variables are no longer in the company's control? The short answer is: you can't do it using traditional brand management techniques—you've got to reframe the problem.

Marketing Automation tools will continue to empower brand owners to actively monitor social media channels like Facebook, Twitter and YouTube, as well as track blogs, forums and online communities where conversations about the brand may occur. Whether the conversation is positive, negative, humorous, or just sarcastic, you must track the sources of such content and gauge the sentiment and underlying emotions in order to protect and enhance reputation.

The key to making the transition from brand to reputation management lies on the examination of the company through a set of "filters" designed to gauge how you are shifting from a reliance on the traditional art of persuasion to the adoption of the disciplines of authenticity, as represented in the image below.

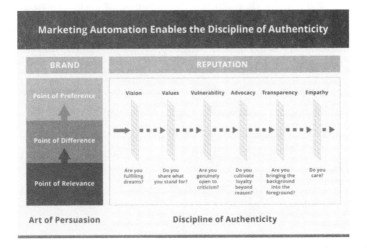

Systems must be deployed to monitor, segment and target the peer-to-peer conversations that represent the highest opportunity and/or risk to brand reputation. When engaging a target audience member, marketing must be transparent with regard to their affiliation with the brand and authentic in their delivery and tone. Disingenuous party-crashers are quickly exposed and ejected from the dialog with serious brand reputation consequences.

This is where Marketing Automation will make a huge difference: unifying social media listening functionality with structured and disciplined customer response strategies. "Reputation filters" will be fully programmable—reflecting the values and voice of the brand and engaging the target audience with vulnerability, transparency and empathy.

Keep in mind that true authenticity is not a destination or an end-state—it is a discipline that must be enforced day-to-day within a company and we believe that Marketing Automation will be a critical enabler for success.

From Campaigns to Conversations

The multitude of channels and technologies for communicating with the marketplace will continue revolutionizing the work of marketing. Today, the effectiveness of conventional outbound marketing campaigns is limited. In 2020, building brands and driving revenue growth will require tools that enable marketers to facilitate continuous, relevant and meaningful conversations with customers.

Traditional outbound marketing campaigns demarcated by periodic sales seasons, budget cycles and responses to competitor moves will be insufficient to engage customers. If you keep thinking about marketing campaigns as your one-shot at broadcasting promotional content, you will miss the bigger opportunity to connect with customers.

By contrast, conversations are continuous, adaptive, and ad hoc. They take advantage of the immediacy and reach of social media channels to communicate with an audience repeatedly and meaningfully, targeting messages by media type and inviting the recipients not just to listen, but to engage with and respond to your valuable content.

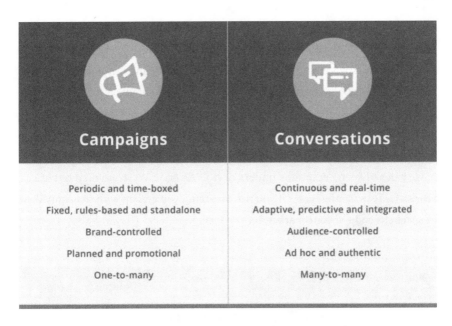

Campaigns	Conversations
Periodic and time-boxed	Continuous and real-time
Fixed, rules-based and standalone	Adaptive, predictive and integrated
Brand-controlled	Audience-controlled
Planned and promotional	Ad hoc and authentic
One-to-many	Many-to-many

The goal of conversation is not just to promote the brand, but rather to engage the customer. What the company says in the conversation should stand out and make sense, but just as important is **how well the company listens** and makes sense of what the market is saying.

We've stressed the contrast between campaigns and conversations to call attention to the challenges and opportunities associated with the latter. As a practical matter, the two should go hand in hand. Any marketing campaign today should incorporate and encourage ongoing conversation with customers and analysis of these conversations should reveal opportunities for innovative campaigns.

In 2020, brand owners will recognize that they can't possibly control the myriad of conversations about their brands. Moreover, unlike campaigns, conversations are often not even initiated by the brand. The most successful marketers will expect their marketing automation tools to enable that conversation both internally and externally so they can engage their customers with the right things in the right way at the right time to drive results. To address this opportunity, Marketing Automation vendors will begin integrating Smart Bots and Intelligent Agent technologies into their platforms to manage continuous, real-time conversations with customers.

From Rules to Algorithms

As anyone who spends a little time with it knows, Marketing Automation requires you to think like a software engineer and, given the complexity of ever-more-sophisticated multi-step campaigns and behaviorally-triggered decision logic — as depicted in the example below — things can get out of hand pretty quickly!

As time goes by, we encounter more and more exceptions and start making more rules to keep exceptions under control. As Isaac Wyatt pointed out at last year's MarTech Conference: "If you're not careful, you end up with the equivalent of spaghetti code in your marketing."

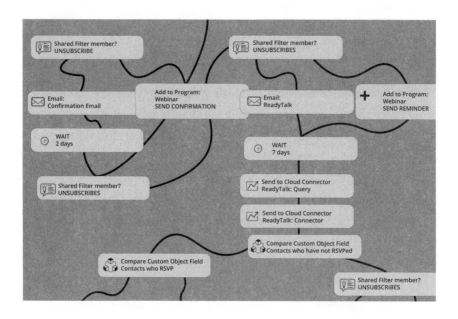

Fast forward to 2020, mature Marketing Automation leaders might find themselves struggling with unwieldy and cumbersome "rules management" processes—especially as the data changes faster than one can keep up with the rules.

We see a tremendous opportunity for MarTech innovators to establish the best practices to tame this burgeoning complexity and then to fundamentally create a better solution. The introduction of Machine Learning will be a game-changer—giving Marketing Automation software the ability to learn, grow and change without being explicitly configured or programmed by users.

Simply put, machine learning will remove the manual task of classifying and tweaking rules each time new information is captured about a customer. Marketing Automation platforms equipped with machine learning will help marketers with real-time segmentation of customers, personalization of messaging, forecasting of customer lifetime value and prediction of churn.

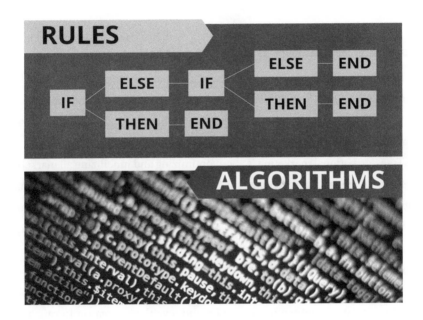

Machine learning combines science, statistics and analytics to make predictions based on patterns discovered in data. As opposed to rule-based decision systems, which follow an explicit set of "if-then-else" instructions known by the developers in advance, machine learning algorithms are designed to analyze data and discover patterns that people cannot find by themselves. In other words, machine learning leverages the massive power and objectivity of computers to see things in big data that slow and biased humans cannot see, enabling the use of insights to accurately predict results.

Marketing Automation Enables Smarter Marketing

Without machine learning, it is simply too difficult to compile and process the huge amounts of data coming from multiple sources (e.g., website visits, mobile app interactions, purchase transactions and product reviews). However, when all of this data is made available to marketing platforms programmed to perform data mining and machine learning, very timely, accurate and profitable predictions can be made.

Marketing Technology Transforms Marketing

Today, MarTech has proven that it can be an amazing set of tools for enabling marketing success. By 2020, we predict that MarTech innovation will literally transform how your customer experiences your brand, converses with you, and dynamically interacts with you.

Transformational marketing is about optimizing and mobilizing all marketing assets to create lasting preference for the brand, to activate customer purchase intent, and to accelerate organic growth of revenues and profits. To truly transform and interrupt marketing as usual, marketers must get all 3S's right: the right Story, the right Strategy, and the right Systems, all measured through the lens of Simplicity, Clarity and Alignment.

Mastery of the 3S's gives you a powerful capability to capture the customer's attention, create an authentic connection and give them a reason to care and a reason to listen. Provided that your brand story resonates with the recipient's needs and wants, you'll give them a reason to engage. If the experience you create for them based on your brand story is remarkable, you'll give them a reason to buy, and most importantly, a reason to stay.

To paraphrase Benjamin "Uncle Ben" Parker, the overshadowing figure in Peter Parker's life in the Spider-Man comic book series, "You must remember that *with great transformational marketing power comes great responsibility!*"

No one wants to be interrupted. Or 'talked at.' Or 'sold to.' We seek authentic. We expect relevant. And we want it only when we are ready for it. This calls for marketing to make a change: a change in how customers understand you, engage with you and experience you.

No longer is the story simply about you and what you offer. Your brand, your products, your services are not really the hero. The power and impact of your brand, your product, your services and your story comes from making the customer the hero, and you, the marketer, serving as the guide on their buying journey

This is called Transformational Marketing.

Acknowledgments

This book is the result of relentless hard work on the part of many talented people. While conducting research for the book and developing content, I had the pleasure of working with some of the most talented and transformative marketers in industry today. Their success became the foundation for this book.

I must start by warmly acknowledging the generosity of these professionals who let me be a part of their story: Mike Ziegler at Ameritox; David Marks at Asurion; Jim Brady and Harmandeep Singh at the Brady Family of Companies; Lidia Frayne at Dell; Chad Thevenot and Scott Barton at IHS; Scott Klinger at First Data; and Kelly Chmielewski and Andrea Koslow at PBS.

Finding untold stories can be challenging, so I'd like to acknowledge Gretel Going for connecting me with the marketing team at Albert and for introducing me to the wonderful marketers at Evisu and Harley Davidson NYC.

I would like to thank everyone at TopRight for their dedication to transforming marketing with our clients around the globe. I would like to especially thank those colleagues who dedicated their personal time, of which there's never enough, on the book. They've added content, been there to think through new ideas, and helped me to bring it all together.

Thanks to Will Allred, Rob Carter, Lisa Cronin, Francesca Figari, Bill Fasig, Siva Kandaswamy, Deborah Kuo and Feyikemi Oniyitan for their energy, ideas and general passion for great marketing. And, thanks to Erin Cribb and Lillian Shaw for their creativity and patience in helping to develop and organize the graphical content.

Of course, even books about marketing need to be marketed. A special thanks to Jordan Blum, Emily Shay and Bill Stone for their help in applying all of the principles held within to getting this book into your hands.

Special thanks to Fernanda Biagini for getting the project moving, pulling together the very first outline and helping along the way with her insights. Also, thanks to the editorial team at Elevate and Mark Russell for working with me to refine the manuscript and for keeping the project on track.

Writing can be an onerous and lonely task. It helps to have friends who you can bounce ideas off of and collaborate with on projects. He may not have realized it, but Brad Power played that role for me on this project – thanks Brad!

To the thousands of marketers, LinkedIn connections and Twitter followers who keep up with my weekly rants on the TopRight blog, thank you! Your likes, shares and candid comments on my ideas is what keeps me going. Thank you!

Finally, I owe a combination of an apology as well as a debt of gratitude to Whitney, Wheeler and Maggie who put up with me during the long nights and weekends I committed to getting this book completed amidst an already hectic work and travel schedule.

Index